# THE EPISTLE TO THE EPHESIANS

# NEW TESTAMENT FOR SPIRITUAL READING

*Edited by*
John L. McKenzie, S.J.

# THE EPISTLE
# TO THE EPHESIANS

MAX ZERWICK

HERDER AND HERDER

1969
HERDER AND HERDER NEW YORK
232 Madison Avenue, New York, N.Y. 10016

Original edition: *Der Brief an die Epheser*, from the series *Geistliche Schriftlesung*, edited by Wolfgang Trilling in cooperation with Karl Hermann Schelkle and Heinz Schürmann, Düsseldorf, Patmos-Verlag, 1963. Translated by Kevin Smyth.

Nihil Obstat: PAUL E. COUTURE, S.S.E., Censor Deputatus

Imprimatur: ✠ ROBERT F. JOYCE, Bishop of Burlington
22 January 1969

The Nihil Obstat and Imprimatur are official declarations that a book or pamphlet is considered to be free of doctrinal or moral error. No implication is contained therein that those who have granted the Nihil Obstat and Imprimatur agree with the contents, opinions or statements expressed.

Library of Congress Catalog Card Number: 70-77601
© 1963 by Patmos-Verlag
English translation © 1969 by Burns & Oates, Limited, London
Printed in the Republic of Ireland by Cahill & Co. Limited

# PREFACE

No one doubts that the letters of Paul are included among the fundamental documents of Christianity. Students of theology know to some extent how much influence these letters have had on the structure of theology, and through theology on the conventional beliefs of Christians who are not familiar with the letters of Paul. Yet this acknowledged place of the letters in Christian belief does not mean that the letters are widely read or widely understood. The faithful who know Paul only from the selections read in the churches on Sundays feel sure that Paul must be an extremely obscure writer; "They drank from the spiritual rock which followed them, and the rock was Christ" is not a sentence of the same lucidity as "Learn of me, for I am meek and humble of heart." Such selections are calculated more to discourage people from reading Paul than to invite them to read him.

This is unfortunate. In spite of the fact that any number of heresies have waved the banner of Paul, it is clear that no one can be anything but a better Christian from a knowledge of his letters. The letters have the same creative effect for the individual person which they have had in the growth of the Christian Church. Our interpretation of the Christ event and of the person of Jesus is still basically Pauline; our understanding of the Church and of the life of the Christian in the Church draws generously from Paul. These are fundamental truths, and they are truths which are always urgent. Why, then, do we not know the writings of Paul better at first hand? Is their obscurity a sufficient excuse for allowing the influence of Paul to come to us mediated by his interpreters?

The Epistle to the Ephesians is neither the easiest of the letters of Paul nor the most difficult. A number of modern scholars believe that it is not written by Paul as Galatians, Romans, and the Corinthian epistles were; in this volume this question is not discussed at length, nor need it be discussed. Whoever may have done the actual writing of the epistle, Paul is the source of the material of the epistle; and it can be read with the other Pauline writings as a part of a single body of Christian teaching. The Epistle to the Ephesians lacks the intense personal impact of Galatians and the Corinthian letters, and it does not rise to the stately grandeur of Romans. It is without the warmth of most of the Pauline letters, and it does not reflect an immediate and real crisis. These differences make Ephesians less obscure, but they also make it less colorful. It approaches more than any other letter something which Paul never wrote: a synthesis of the teaching of Paul. Because it is more objective and less personal, it has less of the involved and highly charged sentences of Paul than other letters; but when such sentences occur, they are difficult, and the reader must pause when he meets them.

I said that Ephesians was not written to meet an immediate and particular crisis, but it was written to meet a need. There occurred in the early Church a heresy called Gnosticism. That this heresy existed in the first century is not certain, but its roots go deep into Judaism and Hellenism and the Oriental cults of the Hellenistic world. Scholars believe that a mysterious belief something like later Gnosticism arose to menace the churches of Asia Minor, of which Ephesus was one. Gnosticism is an old heresy, but like most heresies it never really died; it changed its form and survived, and some of its forms are quite recent. Gnosticism conceived of the saving work of God as revelation rather than as salvation, and the effect of the saving act as knowledge rather than as life. Furthermore, this revealed knowledge is occult knowledge for an elite, and not for mankind at large. Knowledge is communicated to man through a complex system of beings intermediary between God and man, so that ultimately it is not God who is the object of knowledge and of cult but some one or all of these intermediate beings; man does not really attain God in Gnosticism. But when man does realize his final destiny, he does it by ceasing to be human; for Gnosticism denied any genuine relation between spiritual reality and the material components of human existence. The revelation which it prized so highly was in the last analysis irrelevant to the conditions of human life, which are left unchanged by the knowledge of God.

This sketch describes Gnosticism fullblown, and not in the germinal form in which we think it appeared in Asia Minor. But the response of Paul anticipated the fullblown form of Gnosticism, and it answers Gnosticism both in its ancient and in its modern forms. Paul affirms the existing reality of the Risen Christ living in the Church. The Incarnation is the execution in history of the saving power and will of the Father. The Christ event in its fullness includes the historical reality of the Church; and the implications of this reality for the life of Christians are set forth. The effect of the saving act is not knowledge but transformation, a new life in Jesus Christ. Paul will not let his Christians deny the relevance of the world; for the act of God has become involved in the history of the world.

From the other epistles it is clear that the controversy whether Gentile Christians had to observe the Jewish Law was a vital factor in the formation of Paul's theology. When Ephesians was written, the controversy had become less active, and it is treated here with tranquility and not in the polemic tone of Galatians and Romans. The controversy opened Paul's vision to the unity and equality of all men in Christ. The will of the Father to save is universal and without prejudice; Christ is no more the saviour of one group than he is of other groups. Therefore, Paul here presents the Church as a single community of faith and love in Christ. It is the body of which Christ is the head and the source of life. Paul uses the image of the body elsewhere; but only in Ephesians does he add the theme of the body which is growing towards the perfect maturity of life in Christ. The Church in the world must grow in the world; it is transformed as a whole, and its individual members are transformed. It cannot be conceived as a reality which, once established, remains static in a state of ideal perfection. One does not achieve the Christian life simply by joining the organization.

It is the purpose of this commentary to present the contents of the epistle in a way which leads the reader to reflection on what he reads. Father Maximilian Zerwick is well known to a restricted circle of men scattered over the world. This restricted circle comprises the alumni of the Pontificio Istituto Biblico in Rome, where Father Zerwick has spent his life as a scholar. He enjoys the admiration and respect of these alumni; the fruits of the mature wisdom and learning which they admire are here made available to a wider public. This book itself is the best witness to his ability to bring genuine scholarship within the reach of others besides the graduate students to whom he has lectured. To reach a wider audience demands not only profound knowledge of the material, but also a sympathetic understanding of the people for whom the book is written. There is a popular superstition that scholars are remote and detached from the business and the problems of the clergy and the laity, and that they like the ivory tower which isolates them from the world. About scholars in general I cannot speak; but Father Zerwick has not written this commentary in an ivory tower. The conviction is now widespread that the renewal of the life of the faithful in this generation must be based on sound contemporary learning. Father Zerwick is an authentic representative of this learning.

The translation of German is never an easy task, even when the German is as simple and lucid as Father Zerwick writes. Kevin Lynch has rendered the original faithfully into clear and idiomatic English which does not remind the reader on each page that he is reading a translation. Author and translator have cooperated to open to the English-speaking public the wealth of apostolic teaching which the Epistle to the Ephesians contains. Certainly no renewal of the Christian life can be conceived which will not be based on the central themes of this epistle. This work makes it possible for the serious reader to reflect on these themes as Paul proposed them.

JOHN L. MCKENZIE, S.J.

# INTRODUCTION

## The Mystery of the Church

The so-called Epistle to the Ephesians belongs to the group of the Epistles of the Captivity. Its close kinship in content and form with the Epistle to the Colossians suggests that it was written soon after this, probably from the first Roman captivity (61-63). Since it is addressed to Christians whom the Apostle did not know personally, the original recipients of the epistle were pretty certainly not the faithful of Ephesus (where Paul had worked for three years), but communities in the hinterland of Ephesus, most probably in the valley of the Lycos River, where, besides Colossae, we know of churches in Hierapolis and Laodicaea.

The occasion of the epistle was furnished by certain spiritual movements of an early Jewish-Gnostic type, which also occasioned the Epistle to the Colossians. An exaggerated cult of " powers " or angels was endangering there the exclusive primacy of Christ in the work of creation as of redemption, and it gave the Apostle the opportunity of showing once more in its full light precisely this absolute superiority of Christ. If this is true above all of the Epistle to the Colossians, still, this fundamental idea continues to make itself felt powerfully in the Epistle to the Ephesians, where it is especially concentrated on the following train of thought: Christ, the head of the Church, of the *one* Church of Jews and Christians, which he builds up for himself as his body, to which he weds himself as its bridegroom, which he fills with the whole fullness of his divine life, with which and through which he enters on his lordship, not only over mankind, but over the All of creation. Hence the Epistle to the Ephesians has rightly been called the epistle of the Church. In it, the theological thinking of Paul reaches its highest level and its richest development. As a new survey of the reality of the Christian revelation, the Epistle to the Ephesians has the same importance for this later period, as the so-called " older " epistles of Paul have for the time of the Epistle to the Romans.

But along with this basic movement of thought, the Epistle to the Ephesians offers us a deep insight into the whole life of faith in the Apostle. An effort to analyze this life of faith leads us to note, on God's part, the threefold cooperation of the Father, Son, and Holy Spirit, and on man's part his response to God's action in faith, hope, and love. Here a brief preliminary survey will be useful.

The very first sentence of the opening hymn begins with the triad, Father, Son, and Holy Spirit: " Blessed be . . . the *Father* . . . , who has blessed us with every *spiritual* blessing in *Christ*." This threefold action of God finds even clearer expression in the sentence, " Through Christ we have access . . . in one Spirit to the Father " (2:18), and again—with reference to the central idea of the Church: " In Christ you will be built up to be the temple of God in the Spirit " (2:22). Such statements, however, also make it clear that St. Paul is not concerned—from the point of view of theology—with the oneness of being in the divine persons, but—from the point of view of the process of salvation—with their place in God's salvific work for man.

There *the Father* towers supreme above all. He has in his love planned the work of salvation from eternity, and his glory, " the praise of the glory of his grace," is the final end of this activity for all eternity (1:6. 12. 14; 2:7). However, inseparably united to this is the center of all this planning, realization, and fulfillment, Christ the Lord who is the mediator. For an example of these two points, one may consider how in the great synthesis of the opening hymn, for eight tightly packed verses (1:3-10), the Father alone is the author of the action. An eightfold activity is ascribed to him, and yet at the same time the Son is mentioned expressly six times, as being the one through whom and in whom all this is done.

Beside Father and Son the Holy Spirit is undoubtedly less to the fore. And yet in this epistle he is spoken of more insistently perhaps than elsewhere in the epistles of Paul, so that one could rightly say that a Pentecostal wind blows through this epistle. At the end of the hymn, the Holy Spirit appears as the seal of God upon the faithful, "the pledge of our inheritance," the great gift of messianic times, as had been announced by the prophets (1:13-14). Further on in the epistle it is he through whom the Father grants the knowledge of faith and revelation (1:17; 3:5). It is he who brings the members of Christ together into one body (2:18); he is the soul in this body (4:7), the force which builds up the temple of God (2:22), the source of power for spiritual growth (3:16); and he is furthermore the very personal guest of the soul, whom we must be careful not to grieve (4:30). The faithful must "fill" themselves with him, and indeed be inebriated with him. It is the Spirit who turns the word of God into a sword in the spiritual struggle (6:17).

That, therefore, is the trinitarian structure of the reality of faith, in which we live, and to which we answer in faith and hope and love.

By faith are we saved (2:8), by faith Christ dwells in us (3:17).

This thought is found everywhere in Paul. But what is peculiar to the Epistle to the Ephesians (as indeed to the Epistles of the Captivity in general) is the noticeable emphasis which Paul lays on an ever deeper *knowledge* of faith. This is seen as early as the opening hymn (1:8-9), where among the blessings of God, and which is put on the same level as elections, sonship of God, redemption, and forgiveness of sins, we read of the grace which has been superabundantly bestowed upon us in the form of wisdom and insight: God has initiated us into his design of bringing everything together in Christ as head. Twice in this epistle Paul prays for his faithful, and both times he asks for knowledge. He begs for them a spirit of wisdom and revelation, and " brightly illuminated eyes of the heart," in order that they may know how it is with our hope (1:17-19). This occurs right at the beginning. And then once more, at 3:16-19, we find it again, where the highest goods, the power of the Spirit, the indwelling of Christ, perfect charity, are prayed for, but only as the presuppositions of a perfect knowledge of the mystery of Christ and his love. Indeed, Paul expects of this knowledge that it will fill the faithful with the whole fullness of God.

Now in the Epistle to the Ephesians, more expressly than elsewhere in Paul, the first place among the objects of faith whose knowledge is asked for, is taken by the *good things promised by hope*. We are to know what are the blessings which the Father has prepared for his children as their " inheritance " (1:18), blessings which we already possess in Christ, our glorified head; blessings which each of the baptized, as a temple of the Holy Spirit, already bears within him the pledge and guarantee (1:14). The object of hope is blessedness with God, and it is characteristic of Paul that he says it will be enjoyed in common (1:18), just as we should know it already ever more fully here below, in the common foretaste of its joys (3:18). Whenever Paul speaks in this epistle of the " call " of Christians, the thought of this goal, the " richness of the glory of his inheritance," is always present in the foreground as a dominant element (1:18; 4:4). Thus Christian hope, along with Church and possession of the Spirit, belongs to the elements which give the Epistle to the Ephesians its characteristic stamp.

The third element is *love*. Paul would not have been the Paul of 1 Cor 13:4-7 if love had not been for him, in the Epistle to the Ephesians also, above all the love which is patient, tolerant, forgiving and sacrificing (4:32—5:2), of which the indispensable supposition is humility, that is, self-forgetfulness (4:2). This is the selflessness of one who, having been superabundantly enriched by his calling, can lightheartedly renounce all the little claims and satisfaction of the ego. But there is a facet which is more or less proper to this epistle. This is the emphasis with which love is recommended as the power which " strives earnestly to preserve the unity of the Spirit " (4:3), and can make sacrifices for the sake of peace, which is Christ (4:3; 2:14). This is, so to speak, the negative side: the effort to " preserve the unity of the Spirit " (4:3). But beyond that, love, as a positive effort, is every vital activity in the body of Christ, which Christ himself, properly speaking, uses, to give growth to his body and to build it up (4:16). Love appears, therefore, as the natural consequence and exigence, which result from the central truths of the epistle: namely, that we are all one body in Christ, one with one another, one with Christ, and through Christ united to God. Love, in the eyes of Paul, means nothing else but doing justice to this all-embracing reality, living and following out this truth (4:15). The particular exhortations in the second part of the epistle must also be seen from this standpoint, especially Paul's careful exposition of the family life of Christians (5:21—6:9). Where the weak and the strong have to come in contact with one another in everyday life, friction can ensue all too easily, and endanger unity in the body of Christ. Hence the insistent exhortations of the Apostle to loving submission on the one hand, and to affectionate consideration on the other, as between wife and husband, children and parents, slaves and masters.

These few indications may suffice to help the reader, as he meditates on this epistle, to recognize from the start the leading principles of it, and to allow himself to be guided by them.

# OUTLINE

*The Opening of the Letter* (1:1-2)
GREETING AND BLESSING (1:1-2)
*The Body of the Letter* (1:3—6:22)
THE MYSTERY OF CHRIST: THE GENTILES ARE ALSO CALLED TO FULL SALVATION IN CHRIST (1:3—3:2)

I. Blessed with all spiritual blessing (1:3-14)
1. The blessing of God's grace (1:3-10)
   a) Praise for God's blessing (1:3)
   b) Chosen from eternity (1:4-6a)
   c) Given grace in the Beloved (1:6b-7)
   d) Initiated into God's plan of bringing all things together in Christ for salvation (1:8-10)
2. Those who have been blessed, and their way to salvation (1:11-14)
   a) Jewish Christians (1:11-12)
   b) Gentile Christians (1:13-14)

II. The thanksgiving and prayer of the Apostle (1:15-23)
1. His thanks for the faith and love of the recipients of the letter (1:15-16)
2. Prayer in their behalf for the Spirit of wisdom (1:17-23)
   a) That they may know God (1:17)
   b) That they may recognize the glorious goal of Christian hope (1:18)
   c) The guarantee of our hope, Christ (1:19-23)

III. By grace saved in faith (2:1-10)
   1. The initial situation: enslaved by sin (2:1-3)
      a) The Gentiles under the dominion of Satan and the world (2:1-2)
      b) The Jews under the dominion of lust (2:3)
   2. Saved in Christ by God's grace (2:9-10)
      a) Given life with Christ and transferred into heaven (2:4-6)
      b) To the praise of the glory of his grace (2:7)
      c) Saved by grace through faith, not works (2:8-9)
      d) Newly created in Christ for good works (2:10)

IV. "Near" now instead of "far off," the Gentile Christians along with Jewish Christians form the one temple of God (2:11-22)
   1. The Gentile Christians were really "far off" (2:11-12)
   2. Having become "near" in Christ, who is our peace (2:13-18)
      a) He has, along with the Law, removed the enmity (2:15-15a)
      b) He has created the two anew in himself, to be a new man, and has reconciled them with God (2:15b-16)
      c) He has proclaimed peace: access for all to the Father (2:17-18)
   3. Now the Gentiles are full citizens in the people of God, building stones in the one temple of God

V. The Apostle chosen to realize the mystery of Christ (3:1-13)
   1. Introduced by revelation into the mystery of Christ (3:1-6)
   2. Chosen to realize the mystery of Christ by his preaching (3:7-13)

VI. The Apostle's prayer in behalf of the faithful for fullness of knowledge (3:14-19)

1. The "Father of all fatherhood" (3:14-15)
2. The presuppositions for perfect knowledge (3:16-17)
3. Perfect knowledge (3:18-19)
   a) The object of knowledge (3:18b-19a)
   b) The effects of this knowledge (3:19b)
4. To God be the glory (3:20-21)

LIVING THE TRUTH (4:1—6:22)

I. Preserving the unity of the Spirit (4:1-6)
1. The presuppositions: humility and patient love (4:1-3)
2. The reasons for it (4:4-6)

II. Christ building up his body (4:7-16)
1. Christ, the giver of all gifts of grace (4:7-12)
   a) For this has he entered on his Lordship on high (4:7-10)
   b) For the building-up of his body, he grants office-bearers and bearers of grace (4:11-13)
2. The further object of the gifts of grace (4:14-15)
   a) Constancy amid all storms (4:14)
   b) Living the truth, taking on the form of Christ (4:15)
3. Still it is Christ who brings about the growth of his body (4:16)

III. Christian life in contrast to the life of the heathen (4:17-24)
1. Heathen life (4:17-19)
2. Christian life (4:20-24)
   a) Learning Christ (4:20-21)
   b) Putting off the old man (4:22)
   c) Putting on the new man (4:23-24)

IV. The new life in love (4:25—5:2)

1. What love does not do (4:25-31)
   a) Love does not lie (4:25)
   b) Love is not angered (4:26-27)
   c) Love does not steal (4:28)
   d) Love does not sin by evil talk (4:29)
   e) Love does not grieve the Holy Spirit (4:30)
   f) Love does not allow of any malice (4:31)
2. What love does (4:32-5:2)
   a) Love is merciful and conciliatory (4:32)
   b) By pardoning, it imitates the love of God and Christ (5:1-2)

V. The new life in purity and light (5:3-14)
1. The works of darkness and their consequences (5:3-8)
   a) The main vices (5:3-4)
   b) The consequences of these vices (5:5-7)
2. Live as children of light (5:8-20)
   a) Bear the fruits of the light (5:8-10)
   b) Lead to the light those who are in darkness (5:11-14)
   c) Seek in wisdom the will of God (5:15-17)
   d) Let yourselves be filled by the Holy Spirit (5:18-20)

VI. The Christian household (5:21—6:9)
1. Wife and husband (5:22-33)
   a) Wives, be subject to your husbands, as the Church to Christ (5:22-24)
   b) Husbands, love your wives (5:25-32)
2. Children and parents (6:1-4)
   a) Children, obey your parents (6:1-3)
   b) Fathers, be Christian educators of your children (6:4)
3. Slaves and masters (6:5-9)

a) Slaves, obey in your masters Christ (6:5-8)
b) Masters, think of the one true Lord (6:9)

VII. Put on the armor of God (6:10-22)

1. God's armor is necessary (6:10-13)
2. What the armor of God consists of (6:14-17)
3. Request for unceasing prayer (6:18-22)
   a) Prayer is needed, in behalf of all Christians and the Apostle (6:18-20)
   b) Hence Tychicus is to bring news of him (6:21-22)

*The Closing of the Letter*

THE BLESSING (6:23-24)

# THE EPISTLE TO THE EPHESIANS

# THE OPENING OF THE LETTER

# GREETING AND BLESSING (1:1-2)

*¹Paul, apostle of Jesus Christ, by the will of God, to the saints [in Ephesus], and faithful in Christ Jesus. ²Grace to you and peace from God our Father and the Lord Jesus Christ.*

The letter, quite obviously, has a sender and recipients, but let us take care not to have an all too narrow view of the one or the other. The *sender* is Paul, the whole Paul of Tarsus, as he has come to be after sixty or seventy years of growth. But he introduces himself as an apostle, as one who is sent, behind whom stands Jesus Christ, the real speaker, the one who sends him. And behind Jesus Christ is the Father—and that is why Paul says "apostle . . . by the will of God." The will of God the Father in this epistle, however, is always God's plan of salvation, and when it is said that Paul is called to be an apostle "by the will of God," this means that his vocation is also part of the plan of salvation. Nothing could be more forceful in winning our assent to a proper acceptance of the written word of the Apostle than this reference to the origin of his message: apostle — Christ — God. Thus we are brought back up to the Spirit on the very same lines on which the Word of God descended, till finally it could enter our human hearts, —even in the form of this letter.

*The recipients of the letter*: Paul greets the saints in Ephesus, though the address "in Ephesus" is not contained in the best witnesses of the text. It is practically certain, therefore, that "in

Ephesus" was not part of the original text. This is confirmed also by intrinsic considerations, for in the whole letter there is not one sign of any personal acquaintance with the recipients. Now Paul had worked in Ephesus for more than three years. Hence, originally, there was probably only a vacant space for the address. But this suits us perfectly, because it seems to tell each reader or each group of readers: This is for you in particular, this is for all of you! The vacant space is accidental, but the warning that it gives is profoundly true.

*Saints* and "faithful in Christ Jesus," is how Paul addresses his readers. " Saint " has here its original meaning of " separated from the world and consecrated to God." Such, too, have we become through baptism: consecrated to God, united in Christ, temple of the Holy Spirit. This is entirely the work of God, which finds recognition in the use of " saints " to designate " Christians." Above all, the words " in Christ Jesus " are also to be read in conjunction with " saints," for he is indeed " our sanctification " (see 1 Cor 1 : 30).

The readers are also addressed as "faithful." For it is faith (always along with baptism) which makes them Christians. We have to understand what this faith meant to Paul. It is for him a " gift of God " (2:8), and yet at the same time it is man's leaving himself open for the action of God. Only when we grasp this can we measure the grateful joy of the Apostle, as he sees his recipients as " faithful in Christ Jesus " and addresses them as such (see 1 : 15).

The blessing is the usual one: *Grace and peace*. It takes this form because here there is a sort of meeting of the Greek world of the West and the Semitic world of the East, which are united on a higher level. Every Greek letter contained at this place the word " *chairein,*" " rejoice," " joy." Paul exchanges this worldly "*chairein*" for a word which sounds like it, "*charis*," "grace." This is indeed for Christians the new source of a new joy: consciousness of the divine favor which has shown itself so immeasurably generous, and still shows itself so in Christ Jesus.

The Semitic, eastern greeting was "peace," but what was intended thereby was something far more comprehensive than our "peace." It meant more or less what we would express by "best wishes," and signified primarily health and earthly welfare. Among the Jewish people, the greeting was enriched by the thought of the coming time of messianic salvation with all its good things. Finally, on the lips of Paul and the first Christians, the wishing of peace became the wish for an ever richer participation in the messianic fulfillment which had come. It is clear that this can only come from God and Christ; and that it will come is guaranteed by God as "our Father" and by Jesus Christ as "the Lord."

# THE BODY OF THE LETTER

# THE MYSTERY OF CHRIST:

# THE GENTILES ARE ALSO CALLED TO FULL SALVATION IN CHRIST (1:3—3:21)

## Blessed with All Spiritual Blessing (1:3–14)

*The Blessing of God's Grace (1:3–10)*

PRAISE FOR GOD'S BLESSING (1:3)

³ *Praise be to the God and Father of our Lord Jesus Christ, who has blessed us with all spiritual blessing in heaven in Christ.*

Paul begins at once, without any introduction, with a canticle of praise for God's plan of salvation. But this outburst of *spontaneous* praise of God makes us pause to wonder why. Mary sang her *Magnificat,* and we understood why; Zachary intoned his *Benedictus,* and we saw why. But here there is no ostensible reason for such a hymn of praise. On the contrary, Paul writes as a *prisoner*. Let us consider what that means. Apart from all bodily privations, Paul, with the urge of the conqueror in his heart, with the command of God to bear the Gospel to the whole world, with his care for all the churches that need him, has been held fast day after day, year after year, immobilized behind the four inexorable walls that hold him in. Therefore, it is from the midst of suffering and—humanly speaking—from darkness, that this song of thanks is sent up to God. Clearly, the occasion of a letter to a distant, unknown community is enough, the thought of their common faith is enough, to cause the soul of a Paul to flow over in thankfulness and radiant joy. That is Paul the Christian, and that is how he imagines his Christians to be: brimming over with the joy of faith and thankfulness. Let us also have at least the beginnings of such fullness, of that unconquerable joy in the faith, that should turn the most ordinary everyday life, indeed even suffering, into the radiant confession that our Christianity is truly " Good News " and is not merely said to be so.

" *Praise be to the God and Father of our Lord Jesus Christ.*" In itself, tireless praise would be already more than justified by the mere thought of God the Creator. Much could be said about that. But for Paul, the Creator God recedes in favor of the God of revelation, " the God and Father of Our Lord Jesus Christ." What *a name for God* is this! In the Old Testament God called himself, and wished to be known by his people as " the God of Abraham, Isaac, and Jacob." This title was already a tremendous confession of faith. Pascal has described how one blessed Easter Eve he was profoundly and joyfully struck by the meaning of the words, "the God of Abraham, Isaac, and Jacob." They meant, after all, that God was not the cold, distant God of the philosophers, but the God of history, who from his infinite distance stooped down to men, who at a very definite moment of history, in a definite place on our earth, chose men to be his friends, men whose names we know: Abraham, Isaac, Jacob. And then this God, in the course of a turbulent history of almost fifteen hundred years, had mercy again and again on his people, through all their disloyalty, through all betrayal and apostasy—

for the sake of those fathers, his friends. We need to remember this background, to grasp what it means for Paul, the Jew, when God is no longer for him the God of Abraham, Isaac, and Jacob, but "the God and Father of our Lord Jesus Christ." This is the essence of Christianity: Jesus Christ is *our* Lord, he belongs to us. In him, we may call God our Father, in an unimaginably novel sense.

*"Who has blessed us with all spiritual blessing in heaven in Christ."* Thus Paul sums up the essential elements of what God has bestowed upon us. It is strange! If any of us were called upon to recount very briefly the divine gift of salvation, would anything even like this formula have forced itself upon our minds? But it is precisely where Paul astonishes us, where his faith clearly thinks differently from ours, that we are challenged to bring our thoughts into line with his.

Paul calls God's blessing a *spiritual* blessing. The word always implies in his writings an activity of the Holy Spirit, which is bound up with his personal presence in us. Hence we have, in this summary formula of our salvation, an indication of all three persons of the most holy Trinity: the Father blesses us with every blessing, in as much as he gives us his Holy Spirit, and this is done in Christ Jesus.

But what does the surprising "in heaven" (literally, "in the heavens") mean here? What Paul intends is made clear in 2:6, where we read: God has "raised us up" along with Christ "and enthroned us with him in heaven in Christ Jesus." This is the strongest imaginable expression of the Pauline thought, that the resurrection of Christ is already our resurrection, and his glorification already our glorification. For it is the resurrection and glorification of the head, and the head forms with its members one body, the whole Christ. This theme is also clearly heard in our present text, when Paul speaks of "all blessings" with which God has blessed us "in heaven," in Christ. Everything that comes and has come to us in the line of blessing, has in fact as its final aim to bring us to participate in the glory of Christ. Paul's Christian hope is so lively and certain, that he can speak of it as though it were the present possession of what still awaits us in the glory of the Father and the Son. Hence Paul's joy in the faith, which finds expression so spontaneously here, is the joy of an overwhelming hope, assured by the gift of the Holy Spirit (1:14), and by the glory of Christ, our head in heaven. The blessing of God is now explained in 1:4-14.

In these verses, a heart overfull vents itself in a chant of praise and thanksgiving. We must not therefore expect a neatly arranged and well-ordered discourse. No, one thought evokes another, as the ideas crowd in upon him with varying force. But this is no loss, because we can as it were see the order of values which characterized the Apostle's life of faith. It is an order of things which could and should be our rule of life too.

## Chosen from eternity (1:4–6a)

*⁴He chose us in him before the foundation of the world, that we might be holy and blameless before him in love.*

"He *chose* us in him before the foundation of the world." Do any of us ever think of this "election from all eternity"? For Paul, it is the thought that comes first of all to his mind: from eternity, I, the Christian, have been the object of a divine love. There is no thought of any possible foreseen merit on our part. Here the pure liberality of the love of God is at work; and to be able to love me, not just as a creature, but as a child, as a son, with the fatherly love of God, he has chosen me from eternity " in Christ Jesus." That means that I was never in the mind of God except in Christ Jesus; and precisely in virtue of this union with him am I truly worthy of God's fatherly love.

This election has, however, an immediate object and an ultimate object. The immediate object is a truly Christian life in this world. It is sketched by Paul with trenchant brevity: " that we may be *holy and blameless* before him in love." " Holy " means once more being separated from all that is profane and exclusively dedicated to the service of God. And precisely because we belong exclusively to God, our life must be " blameless." And blameless " before God," which means not only in the constant recall of his presence, but in a moral purity which is purity even in the eyes of the thrice-holy God.

But are we not told that before God the angels themselves are not pure? Is not such a demand inhuman? Yes, it is not human, it is in fact " Christian." Or have we already forgotten that we have been chosen for such holiness " in him," in Christ? So we are to be blameless not by virtue of our natural forces, but as the " new creation," which is inwardly united with Christ, which " has put on Christ," which lives from the life of Christ and therefore lives the life of Christ. How should this life of Christ in us, which has been accorded to us, be anything but holy and blameless, even in the eyes of God? Christ makes his holiness ours (1 Cor 1:30). How should the Father not look with infinite pleasure on a human being, who stands before him clad with the holiness of his Son?

It is true that our moral life always falls painfully short of the life of Christ in us, which our ethics should show forth. But our own efforts after Christian perfection, no matter how uncompromisingly necessary they may be, are of relatively small importance in relation to what God does in us, compared to "Christ in us." Christ in us: that is the real object of God's good pleasure, long before we can even think of the ethical demands which stem from it.

Are these demands numerous? Yes and no. According to Paul, one takes the place of all: love: "holy and blameless *in love*." Remark how even in this curt formulation of Christian life, love in its uniqueness is given its full weight! Love is not just one virtue among others. It is the essence of them all, it is the whole law. Without it, everything else is nothing (1 Cor 13: 1-3); with it, even that which is nothing is precious in his eyes, for it is in fact love from his love, from the love of him who is love.

⁵ *He has predestined us to sonship, through Jesus Christ, unto himself, according to the good pleasure of his will* . . .

Paul confirms what he has already said; he repeats the basic truth of our election in Christ, but under a new aspect, and thereby gives us once more a sort of definition of Christian existence. We could render the text of this verse somewhat more freely as follows: "He has predestined us to be children to him through Jesus Christ," because that is undoubtedly meant by "*sonship unto himself.*" One must try to feel something of the supremely personal relationship which is reflected in the words "unto himself," coming as they do as almost a sort of afterthought, and certainly as somewhat superfluous. God wants us, he wishes to have us as his children—as though there was something to be gained thereby for his fatherly heart.

And then comes once more the decisive "through Jesus

Christ." It is not a matter of sonship in a metaphorical sense, as though we were foundlings, taken up—of course, in infinite mercy—from the dirt of the street, and called children, but not being so in reality. No, we are really and truly children of God, precisely because we are children " through Jesus Christ." And once more it is not because he somehow made us worthy of God, perhaps through his work of redemption, but because he himself, the Son, enters into us in mysterious, living union with us, and takes us up into himself, all of us, who become " one person " together with him (Gal 3:28), " sons in the Son," as the Fathers of the Church have briefly summed up this truth.

" . . . *according to the good pleasure of his will.*" Like the earlier word " chose," so too here the verb " predestined " affirms that *God alone is the source* of all this. But Paul has this thought at heart more perhaps than any other. He will insist upon it again and again, and even here he is eager expressly to underline once more: " according to the good pleasure of his will," or " according to the kind decree of his will." (The Greek phrase can, in fact, mean two things: the good pleasure and the resulting will and decree, but further, good pleasure resulting from benevolence and grace.) Paul is intent upon underlining this truth: that the sovereign free grace of God is the sole reason for our election and predestination, for our holiness in Christ, for our sonship of God through him.

. . . [6a] *to the praise of the glory of his grace.* . . .

God is not only the initial source of his grace and its work, he is also the final end of this work. Paul will bring out this truth twice more in the course of this same hymn (vv. 12 and 14). Nowhere in the whole New Testament is it said more clearly, and above all, nowhere three times in the same context, *that God acts for his glory*. He graciously makes known his glory, and especially the glory of his grace, to creatures endowed with the spirit. In this proclamation, in this communication of his goodness, the true self-glorification of God is already contained. The creature, favored and enriched with gifts, responds with such acknowledgment and recognition as befit its nature. In the case of man, the response is his heart's thankful praise, and a life that does not brand this thanksgiving as a lie, but proves it to be deep and genuine and true. This is what is called the " external glory " of God, because, of course, it cannot increase the infinite inner glory of God. And yet God cannot renounce this external glory, because the inmost nature of his creatures demands it. This is what is meant by the statement that God creates and acts for his glory.

But even so, there remains something that we feel as a sort of *discord*. " To seek one's own glory "—something in us rebels spontaneously against it, and rightly so. For in this reaction the innermost nature of our created being finds voice. To be a creature means to have nothing from oneself, it means to have received, and to be perpetually receiving, everything, —including whatever one is, possesses, does, or can do, everything! Wherever a man seeks his glory, wherever he seeks recognition for what he has, or whenever he acts as though he had not received it, something fundamental is not in order. Here our deepest feelings are wiser than we imagine. And even a God who sought his own glory would be liable to the same condemnation, if—as we automatically do—we thought of him in the same way as we think of a man. This is, of course, the mistake we make in this matter, but it is an understandable one, for man thinks in terms of created things.

But God is, in a true sense, he who is "wholly other." If the creature is essentially the product of God's liberality, God is essentially the whole source of all his own being. It is no wonder, then, that the very opposite of what is true of the creature holds good for him. When the creature makes of itself its own proper end and seeks its own glory, the essential order of things is upset. But when the Creator seeks himself, and when he cannot but seek himself as his own final end, that is the inmost essence of his holiness: exactly as it is, on the contrary, the true holiness of the creature to seek no other final end than God alone.

When, therefore, we read in our hymn that God works "for the praise of the glory of his grace," we must remember, in the very moment of the discomfort that may be engendered by this thought, that God is not a superman, no matter how immense we may think him; he is "*wholly other*." Let us try to be penetrated by a deep joy at the thought that this incomprehensible God is our God, who bends down to us like a father and gives us grace "in his Beloved."

## Given grace in the Beloved (1:6b–7)

... [*to the praise of the glory of his grace*] ⁶ᵇ*with which he has favored us in the Beloved* ...

Once more, Christ is at the center of things. All grace from the Father has come to us in his Son, not only in the sense that he is the sole mediator and bearer of all grace, but much more in the profoundly gladdening sense that Christ himself is grace in person. The grace which is spoken of here is in fact nothing else than "Christ in us." But here we have, for once, and very exceptionally, "*in the Beloved*," instead of the usual "in Christ." We may well think that Paul has two things in view: one in relation to God, and the other in regard to us.

*With regard to God*, Paul is thinking of all that God paid, humanly speaking, for his kindness towards us. It cost him his only-begotten Son, in the sense of the saying in John which is so often quoted, and therefore so little attended to: "God so loved the world as to give his only-begotten Son" (Jn 3:16). God gave him into the hands of men, who nailed him to the cross.

*In our regard, however,* this "favored in the Beloved" means what we have already remarked several times: in him, who is the one Beloved, we too have become the object of infinite good pleasure on the part of God, because of our mysterious bond with him. For his Father now can see nothing else in us but the traits of his well-loved Son. What a great confidence should animate the souls of Christians, who know that they are loved by the love of the Father for his only-begotten Son!

. . . [7a]*in whom we have redemption through his blood* . . .

And our sins? Are they submerged in this ocean of grace and love? They do indeed disappear, but not as though they had not been taken seriously. They were taken tremendously seriously. "In him we have redemption *through his blood*." His blood! We are too much accustomed to hear and speak of the blood of Christ. But where blood really runs, men are gripped and shaken to their roots. The flow of blood is like the flight of life. We must learn to pay full attention to the blood of Christ and take it in deadly earnest. For here it stands for the whole historical reality of the death of our Lord on the cross. It should have the same grim reality for us as it had for the holy persons who stood under the cross, whose souls were shaken as though by hammer blows as the blood of Christ dripped down.

The secret of a really fruitful meditation on the sacred text before us, is that what has become stale by custom, and therefore unexciting, comes to life anew in our faith. They are precisely the things which are never " expounded " because it is assumed that everybody knows them. It is true that they do not need to be explained, but the reality for which they stand needs to be constantly brought to light anew, by a breakthrough which pierces the shield of words and thoughts.

This is also true when we hear or read of " redemption," as in our text. For Paul, as for every pious Jew, the concept of redemption was closely linked with that great and basic experience of his people, the liberation from the house of bondage, Egypt. In the Old Testament, God constantly reminded his people, and raised up prophets to remind them, of this great salvific act of his omnipotence. A liturgy, especially that of the paschal feast, served the same end, in efficacious words and actions. But this liberation from Egypt was only the model and image of *the* liberation, whose full reality all we Christians enjoy. It is necessary, of course, to take a deep and serious view of the slavery from which " redemption by his blood " has rescued us. Paul will come back to this matter once more (2:1-3).

. . . [7b][*in whom we have*] *remission of our sins, according to the riches of his grace.*

" . . *according to the riches of his grace.*" Two ideas may possibly be interwoven here. First, this remission of our sins is something so tremendous that it involves, as it were, the whole riches of the grace of God. And then, taking it more theologically: this remission of sin is not something negative. Rather, its very realization and nature is to fill us superabundantly with grace, and to transform us inwardly, so that we now become the object of God's good pleasure. All the more so, since not only forgiveness of sin is ascribed to this richness of his grace, but something completely new as well, in the same breath, as it were. . . .

## INITIATED INTO GOD'S PLAN OF BRINGING ALL THINGS TOGETHER IN CHRIST FOR SALVATION (1:8–10)

*[according to the riches of his grace]* ⁸*which he has poured out superabundantly into us, in all wisdom and insight:* ⁹*He has revealed to us the mystery of his will, in accordance with his gracious decree, on which he had determined in him,* ¹⁰*of bringing about the fullness of time, namely, to sum up all things under one head in Christ, everything that is in heaven and on earth.*

Here, then, is the new gift of grace, which is added to all that has been recounted up to now. God has *initiated us*, his children, *into the mystery of his will*. We were to know how great and magnificent is the plan of salvation into which even our tiny life is fitted. It is impossible to go into all the details of these over-compact verses here, especially as the exact relationship between the phrases and hence their interpretation remain obscure. But the main points are as follows: It is once more clear that Paul is, as it were, revelling in the threefold thought which has already been dominant up to now. 1) The sole origin of the plan of salvation lies in the free will and grace of God alone. 2) It has been predetermined from all eternity. That is what is meant when God " determines " upon something, or more precisely, " establishes his decree beforehand." But above all 3), Christ is here too the center. God has made his plan " in him," God will realize his plan " in him." It is to bring on the " fullness of time." The " fullness of time " here is less the coming of Christ, " when the time was fulfilled " (Gal 4:4), than the whole final process, from the first coming of Christ to his return in glory. This is not only the beginning, it is the realization and completion of the last days.

In these last days, the goal which God will pursue is "*to sum up everything under one head in Christ.*" The Greek verb, strictly speaking, means only " to sum up," but in an epistle such as this, of which the real message is Christ as head of his Church and as head of the whole creation, we may certainly take it that Paul chose precisely this rare word, and used it in a new sense, because in it the decisive word " head " rings out so clearly. What Paul means is made clear at the end of this chapter, verses 22 and 23.

What is to be brought together under Christ as head is expressed in biblical terms: " everything that is in heaven and on earth," in a word, everything, the all. In the Epistle to the Colossians, this truth is affirmed still more clearly, when it is said of Christ that " everything was created through him and *unto him* . . . and all things are held together in him " (Col 1: 16. 17). Here, then, is the mystery of God's will, this is his eternal plan: Christ is to be the head of the universe. He is to give it meaning and justification for its existence, unity, and coherence.

God has made us sharers with him of this his secret. That is, in the eyes of Paul a grace of the same order of magnitude as eternal predestination, sonship of God, redemption, and forgiveness of sin. With this knowledge of the meaning of the world, God has bestowed upon us "*all wisdom and insight*": wisdom, to which all things disclose their depths; insight, in the sense of prudence, whereby we arrange our life accordingly. We are allowed to cooperate with the great work of God. Let us make the little world of our life, the little realm of our soul, and everything that takes place there, the image of what the universe has yet to become. Let us in our microcosm make Christ the life-giving head for everything, the giver of meaning and direction for everything, the center that holds all together.

*Those Who Have Been Blessed,*
*and Their Way to Salvation (1:11–14)*

Here for Paul, as elsewhere for all men, the young Christian Church is divided into two main groups: "we," the faithful, who have come to the faith out of the chosen people, and "you," the believers from out of the Gentile world.

### Jewish Christians (1:11–12)

*¹¹In him, in whom we were also made heirs, being predestined according to the decree of him who works all things according to the purpose of his will; ¹²we were to be for the praise of his glory, we who had already set our hope on Christ.*

The Jews do not stand on the same level as the other nations.

As the chosen people of God, they stand, when seen in the light of revelation, above all others. Paul knows and acknowledges this fact. But this is the very reason which makes it so urgent for him to stress as insistently as possible that this privilege stems only from their being *freely chosen by the grace of God*. How Paul multiplies the expressions for it here! " Predestined " alone would suffice, but no, he adds: " according to the decree of him who works all things according to the purpose of his will." Here God is defined conceptually precisely by his absolute freedom, by what indeed shows him so truly as God.

Just as God is the source of the election of his people, so too is he and his glory their *last end* as well. Here we find, but referred to Israel, the great fundamental interest of the Apostle: all things from God alone, and to God alone all the glory.

And *Christ* is once more the *mediator*. For the sentence begins emphatically with an " in him " which is, as it were, in the air; which, however, links up with the " in Christ," in whom alone the whole universe becomes meaningful. The election of Israel was only a fragment of this plan of God, in the center of which stands Christ. Israel is chosen in him, in him it has the whole justification for its existence, upon him did it set its hope from of old, as Paul expressly notes: " We, who have already set our hope on Christ." Thus Israel was, so to speak, with Christ, was already in its spiritual homeland, before he ever came into this world.

## Gentile Christians (1:13–14)

<sup>13</sup>*In him are you also, who have heard the word of truth, the good tidings of your salvation, in whom, too, you have accepted the faith, and received the seal of the Spirit of the promise, the*

*Holy Spirit,* ¹⁴*that is the pledge of our inheritance, unto the redemption of those who have become God's possession, to the praise of his glory.*

Paul with his overloaded sentences can be rather oppressive. But that only shows how one thought in him evokes another, how they jostle, wrestle, absorb each other in the struggle for an expression which will render as fully as possible all that is living and thronging in his soul. What Paul means to say here above all is this: You, too, have received God's great gift, the *Holy Spirit,* whose outpouring had been promised from time immemorial for the coming times of the Messiah. Now, however, two further thoughts are combined with this main one: the thought of the way which has led up to being sealed by the Holy Spirit, a way which was indeed already the grace of Christ. They heard the word of truth and accepted it with believing hearts. And then there is the second thought, that of the blessed goal, for which they had received the seal from the Spirit. All this is compressed into one sentence, and becomes all the more complicated because Paul cannot forbid himself to underline the fact that everything, the proclamation of the word, the acceptation of the faith, and the sealing by the Holy Spirit, has taken place " in him."

The Gospel is called here " *the word of truth, the good tidings of our salvation.*" The two words " truth " and " salvation " had happy overtones in the world of Paul, for truth was connected with wisdom, and salvation with happiness. Then as now, no, more than now, " words of truth " and " ways of salvation " were highly prized on all sides. We must try to imagine what that meant, when in the middle of this teeming market of offers Paul comes on the scene—as a Jew, with public opinion already prejudiced against him, and furthermore, less than imposing in outward appearance—when he comes forward into this civilization with the claim that he has been sent by the one true God; when, with a courage and a confidence which are not of this world, he preaches *the* absolute truth and salvation. His every word, his whole life is " a good odor of Christ for God among those who are being saved and among those who are being lost; for some unto death, for the others unto life " (2 Cor 2:15f.). Something of the consciousness of the importance of his person and his mission can be heard even when Paul only mentions the preaching as " the word of truth " and " the good tidings of our salvation." He knows himself to be the apostle even of those to whom, as in this case, he himself has never preached, but who have " heard " of the message and so as it were stand within the circle where his activity radiates. What Paul teaches us is a consciousness of our mission, which is Christian, conqueror of the world, and superior to the world.

"*You have accepted the faith*," is what Paul says. We should say, they have become Christians by faith and baptism. And thus they have "*received the seal of the Spirit of the promise, the holy Spirit.*" What is remarkable here is the way in which Paul speaks of the third person of the Most Holy Trinity, who is true God, with the Father and the Son, and is now called the " seal " which definitively marks us as God's property. Paul speaks of the Holy Spirit as though of a thing, an instrument of God. But he is the seal by means of his personal indwelling with his all-transforming power. Are the roles not reversed here? The temple is, after all, for God, and not God for the temple; and here the divine guest is sent for the good of his temple, to sanctify it, guard it, enrich it, and make it pleasing to the Father.

That is precisely the marvel of divine love. Man, who by his very essence is directed only and entirely towards God as to his final end, becomes now in the plan of salvation as it were a center, a focus, upon which the three divine persons concentrate in a certain measure their effort, and in all seriousness. Only the love of God is capable of such an achievement. But Paul in his very way of speaking does indeed take this love seriously to its full extent. The Father alone acts as God, the Son is man and mediator, indeed the price God pays to acquire what is really his own, and the Holy Spirit is the personal security for the fact that we belong to God. Paul would therefore never pray as we do: "Glory be to the Father *and* to the Son *and* to the Holy Spirit." Rather he would say with the ancient (pre-Arian) Church: "Glory be to the Father *through* the Son *in* the Holy Spirit." The struggles for the true Godhead of Christ and the Holy Spirit have gained for us precious clarity and certainty; but now, this assurance gained, we must go back to Paul, in order to grasp more deeply the marvel of the love which made Christ become man and mediator, and the Holy Spirit seal and pledge of our salvation.

But this seal, the Holy Spirit, even as the seal of our belonging to God, is not something at rest in itself, it is an active force. As such, the Holy Spirit was promised by the prophets for the time of the Messiah, and Paul himself points to this when he calls the Holy Spirit the "*Spirit of the promise.*" In his speech on Pentecost, Peter appealed to the prophet Joel: the outpouring of the Spirit is the sign of the dawn of the messianic age (Acts 2:17-21). But still more may we rightly think of the magnificent text of Ezekiel 36:26f.: "I will give you a new heart and I will put in you a new spirit..., I will put my Spirit into you, and will make you walk according to my precepts and will cause you to observe my statutes." It is the promise of a glad assent, inspired by the Spirit, to God's will and command,

and this is what the " Spirit of the promise," the " seal " of our belonging to God, brings about in our hearts.

The Holy Spirit is said to be the *" pledge of our inheritance."* No matter how highly prized his presence is to be, still it is not emphasized as something valuable in itself, but in view of the end for which he is given us. A " pledge " is an initial payment which is security for the whole sum being paid at last in full. This latter is called " our inheritance," which reminds us once more of our sonship of God, which was already spoken of (1:5). " But if sons, then also heirs, heirs of God, co-heirs with Christ " (Rom 8:17). God himself in his glory will one day be the inheritance. And if ever the pledge was of the same nature as the full payment, then so is it here: the pledge is already God himself, only still hidden, the Holy Spirit.

The transition into glory will come one day as the *" redemption of those who have become God's possession,"* or more literally, as the " redemption of God's people of possession." The Greek word translated by " possession " means, strictly speaking, " acquisition," and the whole phrase " unto redemption of the acquisition " has been explained in various ways. It could mean: for a redemption which consists in our acquiring finally the glory of God, in entering into it. But more probably, the word " acquisition " is to be understood as " what is acquired," " property," or " possession." It is, in fact, almost a technical term in the Old Testament when used to designate the chosen people as the " possession acquired by God," " the people of God's possession." Here, then, the basic idea is that the young Church of Christ is the new people of God, which has been bought and acquired by God in a new, unheard-of sense. It will be worthwhile to dwell a little also on the thought of *how* God " acquired " Israel, and *how* the Church, and on how we can feel ourselves so secure and well, nestling in the possessive hand of the all-powerful Father.

But how does it happen that Paul here speaks so readily of the *redemption* as though it were something which still lies in the future? Did we not already read in the hymn, that we "have been given grace in the Beloved, in whom we have redemption through his blood" (vv. 6. 7)? But it is this which characterizes the Christian existence, especially as Paul speaks of it, in its true nature. The great realities of our faith are already present, basically, radically, in their inmost essence; and yet we still wait for their completion only in the future. We have the fulfillment of what was promised, but not the completion. Thus we *are* redeemed, we have redemption in Christ, but it will work itself out in full only on the great day of the Lord. As Christians, we belong to two worlds. That is the difficulty of our Christian existence, but also its great consolation.

"*To the praise of his glory.*" We have remarked the fact that the sealing with the Holy Spirit had as its end and object " our redemption." But man cannot be, as we have also seen, the final end of God and his ultimate intention. Hence in conclusion Paul now insists for the third time on the great truth: just as God is the source for all, so is he also for all things the final end. How then could our hymn end but with the words, "to the praise of his glory"?

# The Thanksgiving and Prayer of the Apostle (1:15–23)

## His Thanks for the Faith and Love of the Recipients of the Letter (1:15–16)

*¹⁵ Therefore I also give thanks, since I have heard of your faith in the Lord Jesus, and of your love for all the saints, ¹⁶unceasingly for you, as I make mention of you in my prayers.*

Only here does the epistle proper begin, and it starts with that very characteristic thought with which nearly all the letters of Paul commence. Only we have here, in connection with what went before, the word "therefore," so that this almost conventional opening of the letter is placed in a new light. The clearer God's work of grace was displayed previously, the deeper must Paul, and his readers, too, feel what a great thing is that faith and that love, with which the readers as it were throw themselves into the plan of God, and show themselves worthy of the blessing of his grace.

Paul had heard of their "*faith in the Lord Jesus.*" He does not speak of a faith directed towards the Lord Jesus, but of faith *in him*, and this shows that Paul here means faith in the comprehensive sense. It might almost be translated by "life of faith in the Lord Jesus," for that is what is perfected so really and truly "in him."

If so, the second element, love, is not really something else, but rather the same life of faith in its most significant activity: "Faith that works by charity" (Gal 5:6). "*Love for all the saints*" is, therefore, something notably different from philanthropy or humanism. It is a love which sees in all the baptized the genuine brothers of Christ. Each one is brother, because in baptism he has come forth from the same womb, and he is united in the bonds of love by the one life in Christ. In this sense, to love is, indeed, really to believe.

Even in the communities of those times, everything was not absolutely perfect, but even something of this faith and love was, in the eyes of Paul, already the sign of God's work and blessing. It is typical of Paul, who invented this way of opening a letter, and who used it as a sort of formula: he sees the good, always the good, first of all, even in what is imperfect, and he sees it as the gift of God. Hence the thanksgiving.

*Prayer in Their Behalf for the Spirit of Wisdom (1:17–23)*

THAT THEY MAY KNOW GOD (1:17)

*¹⁷May the God of our Lord Jesus Christ, the Father of glory, give you a spirit of wisdom and revelation, that you may know him . . .*

Paul's prayer for his friends is that they may grow in knowledge of the faith. The reason for the special confidence with which he prays is expressed in the way he speaks of God, from whom he expects the granting of his request. Paul speaks of him now as "*the God of our Lord Jesus Christ*, the Father of glory." The opening hymn had begun with the words, "Praise be to the God and Father of our Lord Jesus Christ." Many commentators on the hymn feel themselves obliged to smooth out the phrase and leave out the slightly disconcerting article (*the* God), so that they translate: "Praise be to God, the Father of our

Lord. . . ." But the seeming harshness remains unavoidable in our present text, where we feel it strange that Paul speaks of the God of Jesus Christ. However, we have not to make things smooth and easy, but to learn; and to mark well the noble, total, almost exclusive seriousness with which Paul takes the humanity of the mediator Jesus Christ, whose divinity he knows well. In 1 Tim 2:5 we read the forceful sentence, which scarcely any Western theologian would dare to couch in this way on his own: "There is one God, and one mediator between God and man, the man Christ Jesus." Paul thinks and writes as a real Oriental; and hence he emphasizes the partial truth which he has here at heart, with a sharpness and a seeming exclusiveness which makes us shudder. He leaves it to the reader to make the necessary corrections, on the basis of other texts, which speak just as clearly.

"The God of Jesus Christ," in the eyes of Paul, is first and foremost the God whom Jesus Christ, as *the* creature and *the* human being, himself looked up to and prayed to. However, much more is then hidden in the phrase, and everything is directed to making the prayer immensely confident. For he who prays addresses himself to the God in whom we have been taught by Jesus Christ to see the Father. He is the God who has given us this his only-begotten Son. "How should he not give us all things with him?" (Rom 8:32). Above all, however, we pray to the God in face of whom "*our* Lord Jesus Christ" really belongs to us, stands as mediator on our side, and hence can say: "If you ask the Father for anything in my name, he will give it to you" (Jn 16:23; see 15:16).

Paul goes on to speak of God as "*Father of glory*." That is a Semitic way of saying something like "the Father in his glory" or, in the present context, "the Father on account of his glory." This means that Paul sees in the glory of God a guarantee for his readiness to hear our prayer. The Hebrew concept of the glory of God, as found in the Bible, which is no doubt present to Paul's mind here, implies more than "glory." The Hebrew word "*kabod*" means first of all weight, heaviness, fullness, and so *richness*. Hence Paul here turns to a God who is rich, while he confesses his own poverty and need of help. The believer turns to God, knowing that he is so infinitely rich in his divine blessedness that this richness overflows in the form of gracious love and favor.

But *kabod* also means *honor*, and so reminds us of the God who seeks his honor and glory, and finds it in giving. When the worshipper in the Old Testament prays that God may "glorify" or "hallow" his name, he means that God should intervene with his help, and show himself as he who gives, rescues, and is kind (see Ezek 39:25-29).

This is the sense in which Jesus utters the prayer, "Glorify your name," and the answer comes from heaven: "I have glorified it and I will glorify it" (Jn 12:27f.). This is the sense in which Jesus taught us to pray, "Hallowed be thy name," that is, be it sanctified and glorified first and foremost by God himself. When, therefore, Paul addresses God as the "Father of glory," he means: 1) God as the God whose riches flow over; 2) God as the God who seeks his honor and works "for the praise of his glory" (vv. 6. 12. 14); and thereby 3) the silent promise is included, that we ourselves, when God glorifies himself in us, will try to hold back nothing of it for ourselves, but give him all the glory in thanksgiving and praise.

The object of the prayer is "a spirit of wisdom and of revelation." "*A spirit of wisdom*" means wisdom as a gift of the Spirit, inspired wisdom. Wisdom means, especially in antiquity, a knowledge which is important for life, a knowledge which enables man to dominate life. Hence Paul is praying that our faith (and therefore God himself!) may be really a power in our lives, a principle of order. It is to become dominant in all our work and thought, in all our values and wishes. Then comes an effect in the other direction, when action brings about a deeper knowledge in turn. Nothing makes faith more lively than the fact of its being lived (see Jn 7:17).

And "*a spirit of revelation*." This, too, is a gift of the Spirit (*charisma*), one which the Apostle asserts of himself (1 Cor 14:6), supposes in others (1 Cor 14:26), and here desires for the faithful to whom he writes. It is not a matter now of the revelation and knowledge of new truths, but of a subjective realization of the truth already known in faith, therefore a deeper, experimental awareness of truth. Taking the radical meaning of the word "revelation" as our starting point, it is as if a veil were removed, a curtain rises, or—as we say—something "dawns upon" one. It was indeed already "known," and yet it is now like having one's eyes opened for the first time.

The two gifts, the spirit of wisdom and of revelation, are to serve the "*knowledge of God*." Once more, all that can be meant, of course, is a profounder knowledge. The word used here is explained in one place by Paul himself as "the whole richness of the fullness of understanding" (Col 2:2), which we could interpret more or less as the full riches of an understanding which fills one profoundly and inwardly.

But the fact is that in the language of the Bible "to know God" never means to know the existence or the nature of God, as it did for the Greeks. It means, rather, to recognize the action of God, to know his ways and his will. And this is not done in cool, objective concepts, but in a knowledge which is "acknowledgement" and a loving comprehension. Hence here also the "knowledge of God" is merely a short formula for all that will be explained more copiously in the following, as the object of knowledge: the activity of God, and his action in our behalf.

### That they may recognize the glorious goal of Christian hope (1:18)

*[May he give you]* <sup>18</sup>*enlightened eyes for your heart, that you may know what is the hope of his calling, what are the riches of the glory of his inheritance among the saints . . .*

"*Enlightened eyes for your heart.*" It is true that when the Semite spoke of the "heart," he meant the seat of all the higher faculties, including above all that of knowledge. But for him, much more than for us, thinking, feeling, willing, and even doing formed an indivisible whole. And so the association that comes to our mind is correct when we hear of the eyes "of the heart" and think at once of the deep truth which says that without "heart," that is, without love, there is no really deep and comprehensive understanding.

What are they to know? Paul had heard of the faith and love of the recipients of the letter and had given thanks for it. Now he prays that they may have full knowledge of their *hope*. In this epistle, Christian hope plays, in fact, a predominant role. At the very beginning of the opening hymn, Paul had, to our no little astonishment, transposed into heaven "the whole spiritual blessing" with which God has blessed us; and this is what he now speaks of in the very first place and copiously. And once more, it is not a matter of things to be learned. They are already known, even by the most simple of the faithful.

It is not a matter of knowledge, but of an inward grasp, of estimating and evaluating in the depths of the soul, of being seized and stirred by the ineffable hope which has been bestowed upon us and which is waiting for us.

Paul could have said: "what is the hope of *our* calling and what is the glory of *our* inheritance." But he says instead: "what is the hope of *his* calling and the riches of *his* inheritance." The difference is only slight, but it is important. What a splendid hope it must be, since God has called us to it; what an inheritance it must be, since it is God's inheritance! Thus it is suggested that we make God himself the measure of our hopes. One should notice the growing emphasis which appears even in the different number of words in the first two phrases, and is developed still more forcibly in the third member. One feels at once how the thought seizes and overmasters the Apostle.

"... *among the saints*." For Paul, the glory towards which we move is essentially a glory in common, and that in itself will precisely constitute an element of bliss. There the saying will be proved true in an unheard-of manner: a joy shared is a joy doubled. Just as when Paul speaks of the life of the Church on earth, he thinks far less of the individual than of the whole, so too in his mind the blessedness of heaven is very essentially a choir of jubilation composed of many voices.

## The guarantee of our hope, Christ (1:19–23)

... [19]*and what is the enormous force of his power in regard to us who believe, to be measured by the energy of his might and strength,* [20]*which he exerted on Christ, as he raised him up from the dead, and enthroned him on his right hand in the heavens, ²¹high above all lordship and might and power and majesty, and above every name that is named, not only in this age, but in the age that is to come.*

The third element of knowledge for which the Apostle prays here is so important in his eyes that he cannot find any adequate expression for it, but only heaps up a mass of epithets for this "*overwhelming power of God in regard to us who believe*"—which expressions are then expounded upon in terms of what God's omnipotence has wrought in behalf of Jesus Christ. But how are the two things connected? Why should God's unique action with regard to his only-begotten Son be a measure for his "might in regard to us who believe"? Here once again we have the fundamental thought—and it is characteristic that it should present itself so spontaneously to the Apostle—which, as we have already indicated, will be expressed with astonishing daring in 2:5f.: namely, that what the Father has done to Christ, he *has already* performed on us believers. For with the fact of our being baptized into the death and resurrection of Christ, a common life and destiny has now been granted, and it can only be represented by the image of the vital unity of head and members. Only when looked at in this way is it comprehensible that Paul measures the power which God will display with regard to the faithful, or rather, has already displayed, by the power exerted in the exaltation of Christ.

Furthermore, we must take note that nothing new is being taught here. All that is done is to remind the readers of what is taken for granted, as already known. We may perhaps be surprised at the exuberance of language in which Paul's thought has soared aloft. It should enable us to measure (and to appreciate, in contrast to our own feelings) how much the thought of the resurrection of the Lord, and our (future but already fundamental) resurrection along with him, formed a force in the Apostle's life of faith which could carry him away with irresistible power. The "enthronement at the right hand of God in heaven" is an imaginative expression, derived from the Bible, to say that Christ has acceded to the full sovereign rights of God, by means of his exaltation.

We now find it rather strange, however, that the primacy of Christ is still described as being *exalted above all the angelic powers*. This is the first time that these powers are mentioned in the epistle. They will occur again, and finally show themselves as powers hostile to God (6:11f.). These angelic powers are mentioned very frequently in the twin letters to the Colossians and the Ephesians. The reason is that in that region, the hinterland of Ephesus, a false cult of angels and of powers had begun to encroach upon the sole rights and validity of Christ in the plan of salvation. Paul therefore speaks here from the standpoint of his adversaries, perhaps without taking up any attitude himself with regard to the existence of these very powers. He is still less concerned with establishing any sort of rank among them, or developing any sort of doctrine at all about angels. However, the very fact that the angels are supposed to be divided into several classes is grist to his mill. He can thereby bring out strongly the one thought that is important to him, namely, that Jesus Christ, the exalted Lord, surpasses in any case everything that actually exists or may exist on earth and in heaven, now and in eternity. He surpasses, too, the unknown as well as the known. That is what is meant by the comprehensive "every name that is named": any sort of being, no matter how lofty sounding his name, as for instance the names of the powers that have just been enumerated, "lordships and mights and powers and majesties."

We must not think that because these angelic powers are strange sounding, and seem to reflect the thought of a past age, we are absolved from trying to apply this text also to ourselves. How is it with the sole sovereignty of Christ in our life? Are there not persons and things which intrude themselves between Christ and us, and prevent his having "the primacy in all things" (Col 1:18ᵇ) which is due him? We shall never address these foreign powers in our lives as though they were mightier than Christ, but *are* they not, time and time again?

*²²And he has subjected all things to himself, and he has given him as head over all to the Church, ²³which is his body, the fullness of him, who fills all things in all* [or: *who makes all things in all serve his fullness*].

Paul had been speaking of Christ, exalted high beyond all the heavens and all the powers. To express such things, our concepts and language have to rely on spatial images. This has its disadvantages. The "higher" and "loftier" are our thoughts about Christ, the more he seems to recede into the distance. And yet the truth is quite the opposite. It is only through his exaltation itself that Christ has come absolutely close to us. For it alone makes possible that mysteriously real and indeed, in a "pneumatic" sense (I Cor 15:44), bodily unity of head and members. Hence now in this text Paul brings Christ down once more from the heights of heaven and shows him to us, to our no small astonishment, as it were in a fragment of his universal lordship—though, as we shall see, it is the very heart of that lordship—namely, as head of his Church.

Christ, *the head of the Church*: this is a thought which the Apostle has already used in the epistles to the Corinthians and to the Romans. But we feel that in these texts the thought is, so to speak, gradually developing. Now, however, in the late Epistles of the Captivity (Colossians and Ephesians), it comes to take a dominant place in the center. The image of "body" has been fully filled out. The Church as the body of Christ, with Christ as the head, is the most perfect representation of how the Apostle has come to see the Church, after a long life of actual experience of it. Our present text gives one of the most impressive testimonies to the Apostle's conviction in this matter.

The link with the preceding is formed by 1:22a, where an Old Testament text is cited: "And he has placed everything under his feet" (Ps 8:6). The image reminds us of an Oriental king who proclaims his victory by placing his foot on the necks of his conquered enemies. It completes the assertions about the might and majesty of the exalted Lord, which we read in 1:18-21. This lordship is characterized above all by the word "all," which is a sort of summary. The whole *universe*, in all realms and regions, above all the invisible world of spirits, has been subjected to him by God. The Epistle to the Hebrews testifies also to the same truth: "But if he has subjected all things to him, then nothing is excepted, that has not been subjected to him" (2:8). In our present text, the universal lordship of Christ is given a further extension, and a new light is thrown upon it, by envisaging the Church.

God has "given him to the Church as head *over all*." Does that not mean that this lordship over the universe is exercised by Christ as the head of the Church? If so, then the Church would not be in juxtaposition to the universe, the whole reality of the world, nor would it be only a portion of the universe, either separate from it or included in it. Rather, by becoming the head of the Church, Christ has also become the head who is over the whole world. It is as head of the Church that he exercises his lordship over all things. Church and world, the spiritual supremacy of Christ and his cosmic " sovereignty," are all one. This is a bold and powerful thought, into which one must immerse himself deeply, if one is to grasp its force.

God has not only made Christ the Lord of the universe, he has also made him head of his body, the Church. The Epistle to the Ephesians is pervaded by this mystery from beginning to end. The image contains a great profusion of thought, truths which we should weigh carefully, and contemplate in connection with other passages of the epistle.

The first thing that is said is that head and body, Christ and Church, form an indissoluble unity. The members of a body, and its noblest member the head, are a single *unity*. Everyone who is within the Church, who has been called and baptized into it, belongs to Christ—as intrinsically as hand or heart belong to their own body. Separation from the Church, even an inner estrangement from its vital force and the fire of grace, is always a separation and estrangement from Christ also.

Further: the image asserts that the Church is *subjected* to Christ as its head. The head exercises lordship, the other members obey. Government and guidance go forth from the head. Just as God has given the universe to the Lord as his realm and dominion, so also has he placed him over the Church. The way to this supreme honor and dignity followed the path of humiliation. From glory to humiliation, and from humiliation to glory—that is the path of the redeemer. He is the real Lord of the Church, and all visible government and guidance in it, in the words and works of bishops and pope, are in truth exercised by the invisible head. To him, the Lord and ruler of the world, we give our reverence and humble obedience.

The image says still more. All life and growth in the Church come from Christ. The *grace*, and the *life*, which flow through the body, are the grace and life of the head. He who enters into the circulation of this life, he who is in the Church, is ceaselessly nourished, fortified, impregnated, and vivified from this head—for growth in all directions, in the service of his neighbor, for the building-up and the ever richer plenitude of the whole body.

Finally, the Church, as the visible body, is the form in which the invisible head appears and shows himself; it is, as it were, " Christ manifest " in this world. If the Church is the body of Christ, then it enters at once upon the duty which the physical body of Christ had to fulfill in the earthly life of Jesus. It must be the visible instrument with which he works upon the visible world. The inner mystery of the Church, that which is only known by faith, should be contemplated and felt in the members and the visible organism of the Church in the world. A member in the Church, a man " in Christ," and the Church as a whole— that is the embodiment and perceptible presence of the invisible Lord. But if so, then this lordship of Christ must not be lived out in a claim to power, or in the play of forces of earthly politics, but as lordship over evil in its thousand forms. What a task and responsibility for each member of the community and of the whole Church!

Beside this definition of the nature of the Church there is a second, which is not easy to explain: (the Church), " which is his body, the fullness of him who fills all things in all." What does it mean—the Church is the *fullness of Christ*? It could be understood in this way: the Church is his " fullness " because it is filled by Christ, enriched and penetrated by him. But it could also mean: the Church is his "fullness" because it is only the Church that gives him his whole fullness, and therefore makes Christ, as it were, the perfect Christ. Both ways of taking it give a profound sense and contain truth. The only question is what Paul really may have meant here.

The second opinion is suggested by the concept "body of Christ." For here the Church itself is called "fullness," completing, and parallel to, "his body." Just as the head without the body belonging to it is not a whole, and only becomes a complete human being by means of the body, this likewise could be the meaning here. It is only the Church as his body which forms with the head the whole Christ. Many of the ancient Fathers understood it in this way, and many modern exegetes also maintain this view.

The other opinion, however, appears more likely. In Christ himself is the fullness of the Church contained, and it proceeds from him, who *fills* all things in all (members). In this interpretation, the predominant and absolutely supreme significance of Christ is maintained even more strongly. In the Epistle to the Colossians it is twice said expressly that in Christ himself dwells the fullness (of God): "... it was God's will, to cause the whole fullness to dwell in him" (1:19), and more precisely still: "... for in him dwells the whole fullness of the Godhead corporally" (2:9). Thus Christ appears as head of the Church, filled with all the richness and vital power of God, incomparable and unique. As such, he would be the fullness of the Church, which has a share in these riches and hence is totally filled from him. For Paul goes on to say, in the same text of the Epistle to the Colossians: "and in him are you filled ..." (2:9), in him you have a share in this whole divine fullness.

What a *conception of the Church* is this! Three great lines of thought are here linked together: Christ, the fullness; Christ, the head of the Church; Christ, the head of the universe. The dignity he has from God, his significance for the Church, and his sovereignty in the universe are bound together in the closest possible way. Our corporeal Church on our little earth would then be a kind of bridgehead established by God, from which Christ marches out, and which he makes use of, to draw now the whole creation into his fullness, and so to realize the " mysterious plan of God's will." And this would be " To sum up everything in heaven and on earth in Christ as head " (1:10).

Thus the whole universe is ordained to Christ, but the Church is the place in which the universal Lordship of Christ is exercised most clearly, where it is acknowledged and proclaimed. Nothing that comes under the name of progress, whether material, social, scientific, or cultural, can remain foreign to this holy mission of the Church. And no member of the Church can refuse to take part in this immense task, be his contribution ever so modest. Each Christian has to perform his task in the little world which is under his influence. Here, in himself, he has to make a reality of the primacy, the absolute supremacy of Christ (Col 1:18). Thus every microcosm will become a center of radiation, and with the massed radiation of all these microcosms, Christ accomplishes the penetration of the universe.

## By Grace Saved in Faith (2:1-10)

The following ten verses could well be called the shorter epistle to the Romans. The distinctive doctrinal contents of the Epistle to the Romans may be summed up more or less as follows: 1) the misery of sin crushing the whole of humanity, Gentile and Jew; 2) rescue and salvation from the pure grace of God in Christ Jesus, 3) acquired by faith, 4) to the exclusive glory of God. And this is precisely what we find condensed into the ten verses which we will now discuss.

## The Initial Situation: Enslaved by Sin (2:1–3)

### THE GENTILES UNDER THE DOMINION OF SATAN AND THE WORLD (2:1–2)

*¹ And you, who were dead in your offences and sins, ²in which you once walked, according to the mind of the aeon of this world, the ruler in the realm of the air, the spirit, who is now at work in the sons of disobedience . . .*

According to Paul, mankind falls into two groups, no matter how unequal they may be in number or size: Jews and Gentiles. That is not a sort of short-sighted nationalism on the part of Paul the Jew. It is the way that God sees mankind, God, in whose eyes number and mass have no value. On account of its election and the mystery of its mission, the chosen people of God, in spite of its smallness, outweighs by far the heathen world, no matter how innumerable its peoples. This fundamental division still influences Paul in distinguishing Jewish and Gentile Christians.

But while in the Epistle to the Romans St. Paul paints a broad and crowded canvas of how Gentiles and Jews are lost in their sins, here he contents himself with exposing in regard to both of them the grounds and source of their ancient slavery to sin.

The Gentile Christians once stood in the service of the powers hostile to God. They were, so to speak, full citizens of the kingdom of the prince of this world, manageable instruments of his deep hatred of God; and this is a facet of sin, mostly forgotten, which would be well worth a radical examination.

In a language tributary to its times, and strange to us, Paul here says that Satan works in the aeon of this world. The word "aeon" has many meanings, and can stand for "eternity," "epoch of history," "space," or "region of the air." Here we may suspect a special meaning, which cannot be defined with full certainty. This word comprises something which we often call "the spirit of the age." But this would be an imperfect translation, because in the world of the readers of the epistle, the concept "aeon" evoked something eternal, personal, indeed divine. When Paul speaks here of the aeon of the world, or rather, of the world as aeon, he does not mean thereby the world as the visible reality, nor even a particular interpretation or attitude with regard to the whole world. The word "world" is used in a very special way, which characterizes it as a being subject only to its own will, fully contented with its own nature, and therefore in practice making itself God. "Aeon of this world" would therefore mean something like: a satanic, ungodly power, which impels men to look on the world as God, and thinks to hold the world thus in its possession.

The driving force behind him, therefore, in reality is Satan, "*the ruler in the realm of the air.*" The air (indeed, even "heaven"), understood as the lower atmosphere, was looked upon then as the proper abode and dominion of the evil spirits. This lofty position makes them, as it were, superior, and being invisible and intangible (like the air), they are doubly dangerous. They have a lord, who rules over them. He is none other than Satan. We may strip the language of what is tributary to its times, but the great truth remains: God has an opponent, no matter how unworthy, in Satan, and this opponent has power in the world; and in the struggle between God and Satan it is mankind that is at stake.

But we find here still a third designation: "*the spirit who is now at work in the sons of disobedience.*" It is the same Satan. But remarkably enough, in the actual grammatical construction, this spirit is treated as one thing with the air, the realm of which has just been mentioned. The prince of this world dominates and rules the air, that is, *the atmosphere,* in which men live.

This atmosphere is his effective and dangerous weapon—and he knows how to make use of it. It is the air to which the " sons of disobedience " abandon themselves without resistance. This is the air in which the Gentile Christian has to live. This is the atmosphere with which the " prince of this world " propounds reality to man as aeon, as an independent being, that obeys only its own inner autonomy, and finally in fact replaces God. A man who becomes his victim takes the satanic world, so understood, as the end and object of his life. He draws sin and wickedness into his own heart, and there he brings man's inclinations to their full development, and represses his bent towards good. So in the end man serves in a state of slavery the prince of darkness, and harvests death (" you who were dead in your sins ").

That is the murky past which the Gentile Christians must never forget. It is the dark background against which the light of salvation can shine with double force, a source of constantly renewed joy and brimming gratitude.

### The Jews under the Dominion of Lust (2:3)

³*Among them [sins, or the sons of disobedience?] we, too, have once lived in the lusts of our flesh; we did what the flesh*

*demanded and our self-willed notions, and were by nature children of wrath like all others.*

Once more the Apostle goes to the root of sin. But here, where it is a question of former Jews, it is not, as among the Gentiles, predominantly the seductive deceit of the world and satanic powers which make use of them. For the Jew knows the ways of God, and he knows his will in the Law. He yields rather to the allies on which the world and Satan can count in the inmost parts of man. These allies are here called the "*lusts of the flesh.*"

For Paul, however, the concept " flesh " contains far more than we at once think of when we speak of the sins of the flesh. Flesh means for him the whole man, in so far as, left to himself, and being son and heir of the fallen father of our race, he " is inclined to evil from his youth " (Gen 6:5).

Where is the radical weakness of this man to be found? It consists in his not being naturally conscious of his incalculable dependence upon God, which surpasses all understanding. Hence he is always tempted to make his own ego the measure, the center, and the goal, in all his thinking, longing, and action. We could therefore best translate " flesh " in the Pauline sense as the natural *self-seeking* of fallen man. But if this contraction into one's self is the root source of all sin, then everything should be welcome that can help us to seek only God and Christ and to serve them in our lives.

". . . *by nature children of wrath* " clearly does not mean here primarily " from birth," in the sense of original sin. It means the impossibility, part of our very nature, as it were, of escaping sin, and hence the wrath of God, by means of the mere powers of our fallen nature. Only when we ask further how this "natural state" came about are we led to the truth of original sin. Therefore, heathens and Jews, the whole of mankind, are hopelessly subject to sin.

But is this description true? To say nothing of the immaculate one, does not sacred Scripture itself bear witness to the holy lives of an Elizabeth, a Zachary, a John the Baptist? And cannot Paul himself write that as a Pharisee he was "blameless" in the observance of the divine Law (Phil 3:6)? How can he now count himself among all the other children of wrath, who have passed their lives in the "lusts of the flesh"? The answer is: here, as still more expressly in the Epistle to the Romans, it *looks* as if Paul drew his proofs for the universal sinfulness of mankind from experience and from the pages of history. But such a "proof" is, of course, impossible, and fundamentally no such proof is offered. Paul's starting point is always *revelation*. From this he knows that salvation for all is to be found only in Christ Jesus. There is no way that leads thither, apart from him. Hence he rightly concludes: therefore all men are in need of redemption, therefore "all have sinned and are devoid of the glory of God" (Rom 3:23). This is the revealed truth, which Paul propounds rhetorically here, but above all in the Epistle to the Romans, by describing all men as the slaves of sin. Here, therefore, as so often in sacred Scripture, we must distinguish between the truth which the sacred writer means to express, and the manner in which he propounds it.

Paul has described the *dark background*. This he is glad to do. Clearly, he thinks it important that his faithful should have their initial state very vividly before their eyes—how hopeless it was from the human point of view. And we can understand why. Without consciousness of sin, there can be no sense of the need of redemption, without need of redemption no joy of redemption, without joy of redemption no truly glad tidings. If we have no joy, peace, and happiness to offer men along with our words and our lives, then our Christianity and our message lack power of penetration. That, no doubt, is why Paul keeps on coming back to our initial situation, which was, humanly speaking, desperate. And he does so especially whenever, as in the preceding, he has spoken with real warmth, as he discoursed on all that God has bestowed upon us in Jesus Christ.

## Saved in Christ by God's Grace (2:4-10)

### GIVEN LIFE WITH CHRIST AND TRANSFERRED INTO HEAVEN (2:4-6)

*⁴But God, who is rich in mercy, on account of the great love with which he loved us, ⁵ has taken us, who were dead in our sins, and brought us to life with Christ—by grace are you saved! —⁶and has raised us up with him and enthroned us with him in heaven, in Christ Jesus.*

The initial situation of Gentiles and Jews has been described: they were lost without hope of rescue. And now comes the change. " But God," yes, he alone can help us here, and he has helped us. But we must note how every word of the Apostle emphasizes the exclusively gratuitous character of this divine intervention: " God, who is merciful," " on account of his great love," " we who were dead "—and that is not merely a death which consists in the absence of life. It is a death which consists in separation from God, indeed, in enmity against him. Here we can hear the thought of the Epistle to the Romans: " But

God shows his love for us because Christ, while we were yet sinners, died for us . . . while we were still his enemies, he has reconciled us through the death of his Son " (Rom 5 : 8f.). Truly, there was nothing in us that could have attracted God's love. But that is precisely the love of God. It does not need to be aroused, like human love, by the attractiveness of the object. The love of God creates the lovableness of its object. Man is not loved by God, because he is lovable, but he becomes lovable by the fact that God loves him.

"*. . . brought us to life with Christ.*" So much of the wonderful works of God, the incomprehensible blessing of the incarnation, crucifixion, and resurrection, our baptism as share in all this, is compressed into these words for Paul, so that his thoughts are, so to speak, thrown out of gear, and he must break off. Such interruptions are frequent in his writings, but not in the form of an interjection, such as is found here. A pressure has built up in him, and he must give it vent; he has to stir his readers' hearts. They must be brought sharply up against the thought which is all-important to him: " By grace are you saved."

" *Saved.*" This is something that one must have experienced. One must have once been literally snatched from certain death, in order to feel in the inmost fibers of one's being what it means to be " saved "—even if it were only being spared for this poor, brief life on earth. If we really wish to make the word of God live for us, we must try to gather in the school of life such experiences as will allow us to fill with new vividness many concepts which have grown pale and colorless, as for instance the notion here of " being saved." One might perhaps think of the rescue services after traffic accidents. Life is full of telling examples, and Jesus has shown us in his parables how we may make use of everyday life to deliver God's message.

So much for the word " saved." But the real emphasis in the interjection uttered by the Apostle is not laid on " saved," but rather on " by grace." That is what Paul has most at heart. It is the thought that has inspired and directed his long years of struggle for a Gospel unfettered by the Law.

"*. . . and he has raised us up with him, and enthroned us with him in heaven, in Christ Jesus.*" So there it is, this incredibly bold view of the Christian reality, which we have already mentioned many times now. Our *head* has been exalted above all the heavens to the right hand of the Father, *our* head, of which we are the members, one body with him—indeed, still more, one man (" one person "; Gal 3 : 28). We, too, are therefore glorified in him already. What does it matter, in view of this fundamental reality, if our daily participation in God's glory still remains in the state of hope for us? For it is guaranteed by the presence of the Holy Spirit in person, who is already really in our possession, " the pledge of our inheritance " (1 : 14). That is what it means to be a Christian, for the faith of a Paul.

To the praise of the glory of his grace (2 : 7)

*. . . [7]in order to proclaim in the coming aeons the superabundant riches of his grace, in kindness to us in Christ Jesus.*

In the opening hymn, that magnificent panorama of " our Lord Jesus Christ, who has blessed us with all spiritual blessing," Paul has already affirmed three times that the final end of God's action cannot be in man, but only in " the praise of the glory of his grace." So also here : no matter how great the mercy, no matter how strong the love, the final end can only be the glory of God. The immensity of his grace, which was revealed in the kindness he showed us "in the Beloved" (1:6), must be acknowledged and praised for all eternity, with wonder ever new.

## SAVED BY GRACE THROUGH FAITH, NOT WORKS (2:8–9)

*⁸By grace are you saved—through faith. And this is not from you, God's is the gift, ⁹not from works, so that no one may boast.*

The guiding principle "by grace" occurs once more. But now Paul adds "through faith." Finally, there is something, at least, as a contribution from man: his faith! But even so, in the last resort, what is faith but the suppressing of one's self, and the letting of God take one's place? To believe is not, strictly speaking, to "do" something, it is not a "work" performed by man. To believe means to receive and accept what God gives; to accept, in a certain sense, with the eyes closed. To believe means to give up trying to see with one's own eyes; it means agreeing to see with the eyes of another, the eyes of God the revealer.

But suppose someone tries to make of this "abdication," this readiness to be receptive, an "achievement" on the part of man? Paul deprives him of this "boast," too. He goes on: "And that is not your own doing—it is the gift of God." In saying this, Paul has undoubtedly the act of faith in mind. Then he adds something which concerns the whole process of salvation, or rather, the whole process of winning salvation: "not from works, *so that no one may boast.*" Here the whole Paul speaks, as we know him from his "great" epistles, the jealous advocate of "glory to God alone," God's advocate denouncing every claim which man, purely as man, could or would maintain against God.

What, we might ask, is this "boasting" about one's self which is to be excluded at all costs? It is that innermost attitude of man who wills to assert himself, who wills to live not by what he receives, by another's grace, but by what he himself performs and knows and is. That is just what man is, with his inclination to self-glorification, ever since our first parents wished to be "like God," creating their own happiness and thanking no one for it but themselves.

This, too, is what the Jew does in the school of the "scribes and Pharisees" and under their influence. He keeps strictly to the Law, fulfills it at the cost of great sacrifices, and thus becomes himself the agent of his own salvation. He can come before God and appeal to God's promises and claim his own rights. Paul knows this. He experienced it in his own person. And that is the background which makes it understandable how Paul strikes down so fiercely every boast of man.

"... *not from works.*" By "works" Paul understands anything whatever that man performs of himself alone, independently of the grace of God. If man could thereby even take one valid step in the direction of God and salvation, then he would indeed have something that he could boast of before God—a thought simply unbearable for Paul. It would do detriment, no matter how small, but nonetheless detriment, to the grace of God and the cross of the Lord, "who loved me and delivered himself up for me" (Gal 2:20). The more enlightened knowledge of the Apostle is upheld by love, a jealous love. And his profession of faith is: "It is from God that you are in Christ Jesus, who has become for us wisdom that comes from God, justice and holiness and redemption, so that, as it is written, 'whoever boasts, let him boast in the Lord'" (I Cor 1:30f.; see Rom 3:27). Thus even faith is not a "work" in the Pauline sense, for it also is God's gift.

## Newly created in Christ for good works (2:10)

*... ¹⁰for we are God's work, created in Christ Jesus for good works, which God has prepared beforehand in order that we may walk therein.*

It is still not enough. Everything up to now has been affirming the truth that we owe our salvation to the grace of God alone. But this meant what we call the "first" salvation, the call to faith and its realization in baptism. Now, however, the horizon broadens, and the same principle of "salvation through grace alone" is now extended to the whole life of the baptized. Here at last Paul speaks of the *good works of man*. But note how they are presented: "We are God's work, created in Christ Jesus for good works, which God has prepared . . ." Through the whole length of our Christian life also, we are a new creation in Christ Jesus, we are the work of his grace right down to our good works. The way it is put makes it sound as though the life of a Christian moved simply along tracks laid down for him beforehand. One feels in the rather violent statement almost a certain anxiety which takes hold of the Apostle as soon as he starts to talk of good works. He is afraid that this may throw open the way once more to the boast of man which is detrimental to the grace of God.

"*. . . which God has prepared beforehand.*" We have here a remarkably strong expression, behind which there is an unfathomable secret: the mystery of how the free will of man and the action of God's grace can go together. Schools of theology within the Church have struggled hard with the problem, and with each other, to try to throw some light on this mystery, but without real success. It is true that God is the universal cause;

and it is also true that man is free and responsible: two truths which no one in the Church will wish to deny. But one can lay the emphasis upon one of them rather than upon the other, as happens in fact in the " schools " of the Dominicans and the Jesuits. Protestantism emphasizes the universal activity of God even to the denial of freedom. We Catholics are rather inclined to the opposite and so arrive practically (not theologically!) very close to a heresy which has been solemnly condemned by the Church. But many people still picture the cooperation of grace and freedom as follows: I produce the good will, and God gives his grace on account of it. And so the good work comes about! That is precisely the heresy which was condemned, for in that case it would be man himself who initiated things. But it is God who takes the initiative, always and everywhere. Paul writes to the Philippians in unambiguous terms: " It is God who brings about the will and the deed . . ." (2:13). This is what is meant in our text also: " created for good works, which God has prepared beforehand . . ."

To take this truth seriously would likewise be a way to draw closer to our Protestant brothers, at the very point which they have at heart more than anything else. Their basic solution is: grace alone, and therefore faith alone, so that all glory is God's alone. Who would wish to deny that with this solution we are at the heart of Christian revelation (except that this very word " alone " can be, and is, understood heretically). Catholic theology does full justice to this revealed truth. But possibly it stays too much between the covers of books. It almost seems as though we were afraid of the mystery of grace. And in fact it can be all too easily misinterpreted, and then lead to a quietism or a fatalism that refuses all action or responsibility.

The astonishing thing, however, is that Paul has no such

misgivings. On the contrary, when writing to the Philippians, and unembarrassed by the seeming contradiction of it all, he says that God is the cause of everything; he says this, moreover, by way of providing a motive and stimulus for the most intense personal activity: " Bring about your salvation in fear and trembling, *for* it is God who works in you the will and the deed, that you may be able to please him " (Phil 2:12b-13). To sum up the doctrine, which has been expressed by Paul with all possible clarity, we have: 1) God brings about in us even the good will; 2) the object (and effect) of this work of God in us is that we may be able to please him; 3) this universal causality of God can and must be a motive for us to bring about our salvation " in fear and trembling," that is, with a holy seriousness, which doubtless must also involve our total dedication. It is as if the Apostle wished to give only one warning: do not make God's work in you useless! This would clearly be the case, according to Paul, in every relaxation of moral effort. That is why we should know well what it means to be created " in Christ Jesus, for good works, which God has prepared for us beforehand, that we may walk in them."

## "Near" Now Instead of "Far Off," the Gentile Christians along with Jewish Christians Form the One Temple of God (2:11–12)

*The Gentile Christians*
*Were Really "Far Off" (2:11–12)*

[11]*Therefore remember, that you once, the heathens in the flesh, given the name of " foreskin " by those who by reason of an*

*operation on the flesh, done with hands, call themselves "the circumcision"*—¹²*that you at that time were without Christ, far from the commonwealth of Israel, strangers to the promise-laden covenants, without hope and without God in this world.*

The Apostle has expounded a great subject in 2:1-10, the salvific work of God, pouring out grace upon a world lost in the misery of sin. Now, turning to the Gentile Christians, he wishes them to have a very special sense of being twice as deeply indebted to the grace of God, when they now find themselves entering the one Church of Christ, on the same footing as the children of the chosen people. Here, then, it is a matter of the *basically different situation in the process of salvation,* from which Gentiles and Jews were called to salvation. (The moral and ethical starting point, the abandonment to sin, was the very same for both: vv. 2-3.)

Paul begins with a rather external difference, which, however, for the full adherent to the Jewish faith and race was of fundamental importance. The Gentiles are the "*uncircumcised*," while the Jews call themselves the "circumcision." But the way that Paul speaks of it shows him, one might almost say, in a state of embarrassment. The whole thing has become quite meaningless for him in the meantime. He speaks in a derogatory tone of something that only concerns externals, the flesh. It is not he that calls the Gentiles "foreskin." He puts this sneer on the lips of the Jews, and does not omit to indicate that circumcision, on which the Jew prides himself so much, takes place in fact only in the "flesh," and is something performed by human hands. But then Paul comes to the main point, to the real privileges of grace bestowed upon his people, and here, of course, he comes to speak of all that the Gentiles have lacked.

The text is worthy of being placed beside Rom 9:4f., where Paul, homesick and heavy at heart, writes of his brothers, for whose conversion to Christ he feels that he is ready for any sacrifices: " But they are Israelites, in possession of the grace of sonship, the glory of God, the covenants, the legislation, the liturgy, the promises; theirs are the fathers. . ." This was indeed a *glorious heritage* of election and gifts of grace. Paul himself, as a Christian, can only look back upon it with wondering gratitude. In this enumeration of his, something rich and deep still reverberates from the life of faith which the religious Jew and Saul the Pharisee had led. We have to look at the text in this light if we are to feel in turn the emotions which stirred the Apostle as he wrote.

". . . *without Christ.*" They were without the hope of the Messiah, and this was the hope that had sustained Paul and his people and had given them glad confidence (1:12). For God himself had been the warranty of this great hope, God and the history of his people.

". . . *far from the commonwealth of Israel.*" The word " *politeia* " (" commonwealth ") here means the sum total of what constitutes the full life of a citizen: right of citizenship in the chosen people, the duties of a citizen in the theocracy, a life in accordance with the God-given laws. What that meant for a real Jew we can still learn today from the testimony, for instance, of Psalm 118, which tirelessly praises the happiness of being allowed to live and walk in the will of God, a right which has been laid down in the Law.

". . . *strangers to the promise-laden covenants.*" There were the covenants made with Abraham, Isaac, and Jacob, and then with Moses on Sinai. There were the bright visions of the prophets, and the great hope, based upon the promise, of the Day of the

Lord, terrible and glorious at once; while the Gentiles went aimlessly and hopelessly to meet an enigmatic future. *Their golden age lay behind them in a legendary past!*

"*... without hope.*" How sinister and disconsolate that sounds. But there is worse to come: "*... and without God in this world.*" For the Israelites, the one God was everything, after all: Creator and Lord of the world, who gave the world its meaning; and then the God of the covenant, who stooped down in love to his insignificant people, and chose it out of all the nations of the earth, to be his instrument for the salvation of this world.

As one looks back on such religious riches, even the glory of grace in Christ Jesus, as it has just been described by Paul, might not seem too unattainably high; especially as it was fundamentally only the fulfillment of what Israel already possessed as divine promise. But there was not the least trace of all this in heathendom, nothing that could have prepared for the great Now, which has however dawned for the Gentiles, and at one blow placed them on the same level as the chosen people. Raising them from a religious nothingness, *passing by* all the religious riches of Israel, God takes the heathen to his heart, on the same footing as the children of his election! This for many a Jewish heart was simply unbelievable. It was the gravest scandal. But for Paul it was *the* mystery of God, which he is now never tired of praising.

But there is still one question. When Paul points to the lack of all religious values in the Gentiles, which the Jews possessed (v. 13), he is surely trying to make his readers aware of a great lack that is in them. But this supposes that such a lack could be deeply felt by his readers; and is that the case? No doubt, we might give the following answer; his readers cannot feel their lack, in so far as they once were pagans, but they can surely feel it now that they are Christians. They will be able to measure it in the light of the fulfillment, in which they themselves are now sharers. For they know that they are in fact the new *Israel*, and the joy of their possession allows them to suspect the treasures that Israel had once possessed while they had nothing. Indeed, even in Paul, this new Israel may, as it were, have colored and influenced the picture of the ancient Israel. Otherwise he would hardly have put in the first place that "without Christ" which is so profoundly Christian a reaction, and so powerfully charged with emotion. Paul therefore looks upon this Jewish past with the eyes of a Christian, and estimates it accordingly. He supposes automatically the same attitude in his readers. This gives us the right to take this description of a past, which could also be ours, and understand it *in the light of the New Testament*. And we may put to ourselves calmly and seriously a few important questions. For this is the reason why this passage was written also for *us*. The questions would be somewhat like this: Do we shudder—for a shudder would be the only adequate reaction, — do we shudder at the thought of the mere possibility of having to live "without Christ," "without hope," "without God"? Is the law, way of life, and community life of our Church, the new Israel, a proud possession, a source of joy—or a burden?

*Having Become "Near" in Christ*
*Who Is Our Peace (2:13–18)*

## HE HAS, ALONG WITH THE LAW, REMOVED THE ENMITY (2:13–15a)

<sup>13</sup>*But now in Christ Jesus, you who were once "far off" have become "near" in the blood of Christ.* <sup>14</sup>*For he is our peace, who*

*has made both one, by breaking down the dividing wall of the barrier, the enmity, in his flesh,* [15a]*by abolishing the law with its rules and regulations* . . .

Far off—near. It is significant that it is not said what they are far away from, or what they are near to, but simply "far off" and "near," though this is, of course, taken from the text of Isaiah: "Peace to those who are far off and to those who are near, says the Lord" (Is 57:19). This text of the prophet speaks of those who are estranged from God or close to God among the chosen people. For Paul it is the Gentiles and the Jews. Hence *the distance* is what Paul has just described as the cheerless initial state of the Gentiles, which they are never to forget (2:12). It was far from God, from every hope, from every promise, from the broad realms of God's kingship, from Christ, the bringer of all these good things. We must try to feel something of the pain that echoes in the word "far," and something of the joy at being at home that rings in the word "near," when Paul speaks of being far from God or near him.

However, in the light of all that follows, this distance is still, or indeed primarily, to be understood as distance from the people of election, a separation in hostility and deeply rooted aversion. Hence when the Gentiles come from being far off, and draw near, it means the *alliance of Gentiles and Jews* to form a new people of brothers. But further, this has come about through the blood of Christ, "in Christ Jesus." In the new order of things he has become, so to speak, *the* place of proximity to God. He binds the members of his body together, for only the members belong to one another and can form one living body.

That Jews and Gentiles become one in Christ is the great overwhelming fact that fascinates Paul. In what follows, it seems as though he cannot stop himself from celebrating this mystery (2:11-22). He cannot do enough to praise the grace that he, Paul, is to proclaim this mystery and thereby make it come true (3:1-13).

"*He is our peace*." Thus Paul sums up, briefly and trenchantly, the theme that he is about to expound. There follows an almost bewildering mass of images, some of which appear also quite strange, a crowd of thoughts that grapple and combine with one another and make the interpretation none too easy. The main idea, however, of peace between Gentile and Jew appears clearly throughout.

Paul speaks first about the cause of *division,* which the bringer of peace has to remove, in order to make " one " out of two separate things. He speaks of a " dividing wall," which is a " barrier " holding them apart, and whose real name is " enmity." He speaks also of the Law, with its multitude of precepts. It is obviously considered as the basis of this enmity, and therefore it must be abrogated.

The existence of this enmity is attested by a huge number of ancient texts. The Jew could feel only abhorrence for the uncircumcised. Israel alone had been chosen, and Israel alone had kept itself pure, at least in principle, from the horrors of the heathen world, idolatry, licentiousness, and the shedding of innocent blood. In face of this corrupt and corrupting heathen world, there was only one thing possible: separation, inward and outward isolation; and the horror felt at the heathen world was part of this inward separation. It was also sustained by a great portion of the express declarations of God's will, the Law, which with its innumerable precepts, especially about the clean and unclean, claimed so completely the life of the law-abiding Jew, that living along with non-Jews was not possible.

It is understandable that this contemptuous attitude, this markedly exceptional position among the nations, was countered with a corresponding hatred. In a world which was rather proud of its universal " philanthropy," due to the influence of Stoic philosophy, the Jew, with his arrogant isolationism, came necessarily to be regarded as " the enemy of the human race " (Tacitus), and to be treated accordingly. The Law was the bulwark that divided them. If the Law was done away with, the division and the enmity was eliminated.

The Law, however, came from God, and was given in view of binding men in love and obedience to God its author. *How was the Law to be abolished* without lawlessness taking its place? God found a way. He abolished the Law by causing his Son to fulfill it once for all, to fulfill it far and away beyond its claims—not in a series of individual performances, but by means of what was the meaning and intention of the Law: obedience and love. This was what was accomplished and given its unsurpassable expression in the death of the Lord on the cross. This is what Paul means when he says that Christ " in his flesh . . . [abolished] the Law "—not its meaning, but the Law " with its rules and regulations."

And " Christ " has fulfilled this Law in his role of the *second Adam,* which means for the whole of mankind. From now on there is to be only one way to God: to enter, by faith and sacrament, into Jesus Christ's fulfillment of the Law, to enter into his obedience and loving death and thereby into his resurrection and glory. This is, to be sure, a way of abolishing the Law which surpasses anything we could think of as worthy of God and beneficial to mankind.

## HE HAS CREATED THE TWO ANEW IN HIMSELF, TO BE A NEW MAN, AND HAS RECONCILED THEM WITH GOD (2:15b–16)

*. . . ¹⁵ᵇin order that he might create of the two in himself a new man, making peace, ¹⁶and reconcile both in one body to God through the cross, killing the enmity, in himself.*

Here, therefore, it is a matter of a truly *new creation*. This takes place "*in him*." He takes into himself the two opposing camps, and the result is "*a* new man." This is truly a work of unification which infinitely surpasses anything that might be called merely peaceable or conciliatory or even loving. Here peace and love are anchored in such grounds of being as only God's wisdom could design, God's omnipotence create, Christ's love give effect to. The hostile brothers are "a new man" in Christ! How could peace not reign there? Hence Paul adds—as a sort of echo which recalls the memory of the theme—: "[thus] making peace."

It is Christ, however, who has become the "new man," in the resurrection, through the Spirit (Rom 1:4), who changes his "body of flesh" into a "spiritual body" (1 Cor 15:46), and has thus enabled him both to remain himself and still unite the many to him as his body.

". . . and reconcile both in one body to God through the cross." This "one body" of Christ can only be the body of Jesus Christ on the cross. Jews and Gentiles have died in him, for he who hung on the cross already embraced the whole of humanity, since he was the *second Adam*. It is true, of course, that men belong to Christ as the second Adam only "by right" to start with. The actual, salvific, vivifying union with him can only come about when they freely join themselves to him in faith and baptism. But it *can* come about, and it is there for all men. This

## He has proclaimed peace; access for all to the Father (2:17-18)

... *17and he came and proclaimed peace to you who were afar, and peace to those near; 18for through him we both have access in one Spirit to the Father.*

One asks oneself, in some astonishment, what is meant by this " coming," and in what way Christ has " proclaimed " peace. The truth is that he who wrought the work also gave it its interpretation, if not at once in person, at least through his Spirit. The Acts of the Apostles tells how the heathen world came to be admitted into the Church without becoming subject to the Law. That is all one thing. And so *Christ* was " the messenger of the great counsel " (see Is 9:5, ancient Greek version) in the person of his envoys. " Ambassadors in lieu of Christ " is what Paul calls them (2 Cor 5:20). It is significant that Christ is seen here behind his envoys, or rather, in and through them, and that is how his message is perceived.

Now Paul gives another summary outline of what the peace that he has been speaking of consists in: " for through him we both have *access in one Spirit to the Father."* This, therefore, is the peace between Jew and Gentile: the common goal is the one Father; the common way is the new one, Christ the Lord alone; the common strength is the Holy Spirit who, as the outpouring of God's love, enables them both to march along this common way. But what else is this, but to be taken up into the life of love of the divine Trinity itself! And this is accomplished, by virtue of the eternal procession of the Son from the Father, in the very return of the Son to the Father in the Holy Spirit, —in all of which humanity, mysteriously, is to have a part. But we should note that even this sublimest truth is not propounded upon here for its own sake, but as the cause of peace between Gentile and Jew. So too, earlier on, Paul spoke of the reconciliation of the world with God, which is the kernel of the whole process of salvation; not for its own sake, but in so far as it took place in *one* body, and so had unitive power. How often Paul enriches us with these theologically important assertions, made not so much with the express intention of propounding doctrine, as to correspond to some merely secondary intention of his!

*Now the Gentiles Are Full Citizens in the People of God, Building Stones in the One Temple of God (2:19–22)*

[19]*Thus you are no longer aliens and exiles, but you are fellow citizens of the saints and members of God's household,* [20] *built up upon the foundation of the apostles and prophets, the corner stone being Christ Jesus himself. In him the whole building is bound together and grows into a holy temple in the Lord.* [22]*In him you are also being built up together to be a dwelling place of God in the Spirit.*

It is with an obvious joyfulness that Paul launches into the description of the new situation of his brothers from heathendom. The picture is the direct opposite of the religious abandonment from which they came (2:11f.). Everything has become quite different now.

"*You are no longer aliens.*" In ancient times, the stranger in the land was without rights and protection; indeed, the very word " stranger " could evoke a feeling of hostility. ". . . and exiles " : these immigrants were permanent settlers in the country, of course, but in fact they were only there on tolerance, and had no real share in public life.

" But you are fellow citizens of the saints." Two things are asserted here. First, they are *full citizens*. We have no longer any idea now of the pride with which the man of antiquity felt himself as " citizen " of his tiny city-state. It meant freedom, protection of law, the right to vote on all matters of public interest, responsibility with others for a great and sacred inheritance. That made life rich and worthwhile for the citizen of the ancient state.

Secondly, they are not just citizens of anywhere, they are " fellow citizens *of the saints*." Here Paul is probably not thinking only of his fellow Christians, or of Christians from the chosen people in particular. For him, the Church of Christ also includes heaven, with its angels, and the saints who have already completed their course. The author of the Epistle to the Hebrews describes for us the Church which the new converts enter—in contrast to Sinai with its terrors—as : " You have come to the mountain of Zion, to the city of the living God, the heavenly Jerusalem : to the myriads of angels, to the festival, and to the community of the first-born who are enrolled in heaven, to God, the judge of all, to the spirits of the just made perfect, to Jesus, the mediator of the new covenant, and to the blood of the sprinkling, that cries louder than Abel's " (Heb 12 : 22-24). That is the Church, which stands on the earth and soars into heaven, and therefore is called here " the heavenly Jerusalem." That is the state and the citizenship into which the Gentiles have been admitted, as "fellow citizens of the saints" (see also Phil 3:20).

"*... and members of God's household.*" While the concept "citizen" confines us to the thought of the city-state, this commonwealth now appears as the house of God, and so as a family in the true and proper sense. The Greek word simply means "belonging to a house." And now Paul speaks of the house, the family, of God, where God himself is Father and Jesus Christ *the* Son. In him, however, others now are called, many, indeed all, to enter into this sonship of God (1:5) and become children in God's house.

But there is more. A house is a home, and a home means warmth and security; it is the place that one prefers to all others; and it is doubly treasured if it has been given to one gratuitously, as though he had been a foundling in the street. And this is what the Gentiles were, foundlings who now find themselves in the house of God as daughters and sons: "I will be to you a Father, and you shall be sons and daughters to me, says the Lord, the omnipotent" (2 Cor 6:18).

"*... built up on the foundation of the apostles and prophets.*" "House" leads Paul to the image of building a house, so that he can throw light on another side of the situation of the Gentile Christians. Not only are they at home in the house of God, but they themselves make up this house, much like the building stones form the Temple. The first thing that Paul emphasizes is the benefit of a firm foundation. A foundation is surely a benefit, for it gives something to stand and build upon. A foundation means a firm hold and a secure anchorage; it is the opposite of that which is blown about by every wind of doctrine (which Paul will speak about later, in 4:4).

The foundation upon which we stand, furthermore, is worthy

of all trust and confidence, for it is "apostles and prophets." Both words point beyond themselves. "Apostles" are envoys, they are sent by Jesus Christ, and Jesus has been sent by his Father. The apostles are the "twelve" whom Jesus sent into the whole world with the promise that he would remain with them for all time; they are the twelve, but also all those whom they in turn admit into their mission.

"Prophets" is a description of the second group which forms the foundation of the Church. Undoubtedly, only New Testament prophets can be meant here. They are also named along with the apostles in 3:5 and 4:11, and there they cannot be understood except as New Testament prophets. A "prophet" is the name given to one who speaks in the name of God, whom God himself uses as his instrument when he speaks. In a stricter, more technical sense, a prophet is one who possesses the charisma, the Spirit's gift of inspired speech; he is the "charismatic," through whom the Holy Spirit makes himself heard in a special manner: the Spirit who distributed his extraordinary gifts of grace lavishly in the days of the young Church.

"Apostles and prophets" are the *foundation of the Church*, but of course only as the visible instruments of him who sent them and filled them with the Spirit. They are the foundation in as much as they are bearers of the message, which is Christ. In this regard, there is no contradiction with what Paul says in 1 Cor 3:10: "No other foundation can be laid than that which is laid down, Jesus Christ." With the message that he delivers, the apostle himself necessarily becomes the foundation for those who believe, in response to his word.

"... *the cornerstone being Jesus Christ himself.*" The Greek word actually means "the point forming a corner," which when said of the "stone" gives the sense of "cornerstone." Some notable modern exegetes try to explain the word as the "keystone" which closes an arch or dome. Others point out that the cornerstone links two walls together, and hence apply it to the role of Christ, in whom the two divisions of mankind, Jew and Gentile, come together. But perhaps it is better not to think too much in precise architectural terms. Paul takes over the imagery of Is 28:16: "Thus says the Lord: Know well that it is I who am laying a foundation stone in Zion, a tested stone, a precious cornerstone, laid firm and strong. He who believes shall not be put to shame." This is what Paul means, and the point of Christ's being the cornerstone is that he is something uniquely decisive for the construction, which determines its situation and assures its stability. The important thing here, where Paul is speaking of how the Gentiles are admitted as parts of the structure into the house of God, is that Christ is there, with his whole being, at the work of construction. He gives directives, his intervention is decisive, and his influence as cornerstone pervades the whole structure.

"*In him the whole building is bound together and grows into a holy temple in the Lord*." This, then, is the goal: There is to be a *holy temple*. The Church, especially the local Church as temple of God, is an idea which constantly recurs in Paul, and one quite important for practical conclusions. Hence he can threaten the Corinthians: "Do you not know that you are a temple of God and that the Spirit of God dwells in you? He who destroys the temple of God [by disunion and division] will be destroyed by God; for the temple of God is holy; and that temple you are" (1 Cor 3:16f.). The holiness of the temple, guarded jealously by God, there forces St. Paul to sound a warning note. In the present text, it is felt as the joyous goal of our calling, and it gives a new meaning to the life of the

Gentile Christians: to be there for God, for his worship and his glory.

It is well worth noting how the thought of the salvation of the individual recedes so completely here. The Christian finds the dignity and greatness of his existence in the collective effort which he is allowed to serve: that the temple of God may be built, and that it may be worthy of God. The Christian serves it not only with what he does, but with his whole being and person, because he is inserted into this temple in his own particular place and cannot be replaced by another. In all this, the holiness of the temple and of the elements which compose it, Christ alone is the source. This is brought out once more with emphasis by the addition " in the Lord."

It is as though Paul had lost sight of the Gentile Christians for the moment. He is clearly preoccupied by all that this means for himself. For now he repeats the same thought once again, this time applying it expressly to the Gentile Christians: " In him you are also being built up together to be a dwelling place of God in the Spirit." Once more we cannot miss the trinitarian note in the ending which crowns the thought: through Christ, unto God, in the Holy Spirit.

Looking back upon the passage, we may say that Paul must have felt all that he had to say very strongly, since he welcomes with such exuberant joy these newcomers to the house of God, and indeed, even indicates that they are blessed on that account.

## The Apostle Chosen to Realize the Mystery of Christ (3:1–13)

### Introduced by Revelation into the Mystery of Christ (3:1–6)

¹ *That is why I, Paul, am the prisoner of Christ Jesus for your sakes, the Gentiles—*²*you have surely heard of the institution of grace, which God has committed to me in your behalf,* ³*that the mystery, of which I have just treated briefly, was disclosed to me by revelation.* ⁴*As you read it, you can perceive thereby how deeply I have penetrated into the mystery of Christ,* ⁵*which in other generations was not made known to the children of men, as it has now been revealed to his holy apostles and prophets in the Spirit,* ⁶*that the Gentiles are co-heirs, co-incorporated, co-participants in the promise, in Christ Jesus.*

Once Paul has soared into one of his magnificent descriptions of the salvific word of God, he then feels the urge to pray for his faithful, that they may be able to comprehend very thoroughly all that has been bestowed upon them by God. This he felt earlier, at 1:18f., and so he does now. He uses a formula which is not very usual, but which is therefore all the more solemn, and which could be translated perhaps by "for the sake of this." This opening is important because its reappearance at 3:14 shows that the prayer which he had in mind in our present text, 3:1, only begins there. It had been interrupted immediately by a new thought which had occurred to him and which holds his attention for the full length of twelve verses.

To impress his proposed prayer on the minds of his readers, the Apostle underscores who is praying here: "I, Paul, the prisoner of Christ Jesus for your sakes, the Gentiles." He is indeed *the prisoner of Christ Jesus.* No doubt his warders are Roman soldiers, and iron chains may fetter his freedom, but he knows, and it is his deepest consolation: he who really holds him captive, he to whom he has surrendered his whole liberty, is none other than Christ. And if Christ now wishes to have him imprisoned and fettered externally too, he knows that this also is for the salvation of the Gentiles, to which he has been dedicated by Christ.

But that is what he must now add in. He had spoken of the call of the Gentiles, but in this order of things set up by God's grace, Paul takes a place which no one else can match. He is *the chosen instrument,* through which God calls the Gentiles. The recipients of the letter did not know Paul personally, but how could they have not heard of him, since the good tidings and salvation had come to them by his mediation.

Paul sees his call as a *gift of grace.* He will go on at once, in gratitude and indeed astonishment, to call it a " grace," for the second and third time (3:7f.). It is a grace, and therefore something totally unmerited, which comes only from God's free choice and his deep mercy.

The basis of his whole apostolate to the Gentiles is the *revelation of the mystery* which has been granted him. We have already met " the mystery " at 1:9. There it was " the mystery of God's will," intent on bringing the whole universe together in Christ: " All that is in heaven and on earth "— and, of course, including here on earth the world of the Gentiles. For Paul, this is always the same thing as the application of the redemption by faith, and not by the Law of the Jews.

That his insight into the divine plan of salvation has come to him by revelation should already have forced itself on the minds of his readers, from all that he could recount hitherto of this plan of salvation, as he sang its praises. He is confident that they will recognize his grace.

The disclosure of the mystery is the great grace of the present time. It had remained unknown to previous ages, unknown at least in the clarity " in which it has now been revealed to his holy apostles and prophets." Paul, of course, himself belongs to these " holy apostles." Here we may still hear something of the original sense of the word " holy ": chosen and set apart for some special work in the service of God.

It is even more noteworthy that Paul as a matter of course here ascribes to a number of apostles and prophets something which he has just claimed for himself, apparently as a quite unique privilege of grace: the fact of being the immediate recipient of this divine revelation. Now the recipients are numerous, the mystery was " revealed " to them, and this was done " in the Spirit." Immediately afterwards it seems as though Paul spoke of himself as the *one* envoy sent to the Gentiles.

*The consciousness of his call* which the Apostle has, occasionally gives rise to astonishment on our part, as soon as we remember that others beside him were working in the service of the mission to the Gentiles. Even the revelation of the mystery does not explain the uniqueness of Paul, the special quality that makes him different, as it were. For this revelation was also bestowed upon " the holy apostles and prophets." What gives Paul the consciousness of being *the* Apostle of the Gentiles is no doubt the unique nature of his call, and further, the incomparable success with which God had confirmed this call for him, year after year, so to speak, and day after day. Paul speaks as *this* Apostle of the Gentiles, such as he has only gradually become: not as the only one, but as the one favored beyond all others.

And there is something else. From his first journey on, he was a lone traveller. He goes his way, led by the Spirit. He works only where no others have already preached before him. What he seeks in his restless zeal is unbroken country which he can open up for Christ. But there he knows that he is really *the* envoy of God, *the* instrument of his grace. No matter how many teachers and " pedagogues " come after him, these Christians have only one father, Paul, who was the first to impart to them the true life (1 Cor 4:15). In their regard, Paul knows that he is *the* " Apostle of the Gentiles." In the present instance, this consciousness embraces even those who were only won for the Gospel by the disciples of the Apostle, his extra arm (Col 2:1).

Now we hear at last, pronounced in clear and unmistakable terms, *the nature of the mystery* which was made known in the Spirit, as a revelation, to the " holy apostles and prophets." The Gentiles are co-heirs, co-incorporated, co-participants in the promise in Christ Jesus." This had been treated of at length already in the preceding portion. It is all the more significant, then, that the Apostle now feels himself forced to bring out the one truth in ever new guises: that every division and difference has been abolished. They have the same rights, exactly the same rights (that is what is underlined by the triple " co- "), former Gentiles and former Jews, once they have entered the one body of Christ which embraces them both, the Church.

They are " joint heirs," because they are children of the one Father, and brothers of Jesus Christ. Their " share in the promise " is the same, though this promise was given only to the chosen people—so much so that this promise was the only real base upon which the rights of this people to be a people were founded. And they are joint heirs and participants, because the Gentiles are now co-incorporated. What Paul says literally is "co-body," a word which he had to invent. The absolute novelty of what he wished to say needed a new word. Hence we should translate the word as it stands, by "co-body," awkward though it sounds. The Greek "*syssoma*" of Paul must have sounded just as harsh to the ears of his first readers.

## Chosen to Realize the Mystery of Christ by His Preaching (3:7–13)

*[The Gentiles have become co-heirs]* ⁷*through the Gospel, of which I became the Minister, in accordance with the gift of God's grace, which was given to me in the working of his power. ⁸To me, the least of all the saints, this grace was given, to proclaim to the Gentiles the Gospel of the unfathomable riches of Christ ⁹and to bring to light how the mystery is realized which had been hidden from eternity in God, the creator of all, ¹⁰so that now the manifold wisdom of God should be made known, through the Church, to the powers and authorities in the heavens, ¹¹in accordance with his eternal purpose, which he has accomplished in Christ Jesus our Lord. ¹²In him we have been given full assurance and free access, in confident faith in him. ¹³Wherefore I pray not to lose heart on account of my tribulations in your behalf; for they are indeed a source of pride for you.*

A minister of the Gospel, " in accordance with the *gift of God's grace*, which was given to me in the working of his power "! Paul expresses in a strangely ponderous manner something that could appear quite simple to us at first sight. But Paul's way of expressing himself shows that this call to preach the Gospel to the Gentiles was something incomprehensible to him and therefore almost beyond his power to describe. He sees in it first and foremost a gift of grace. And, as though he were trying to savor this privilege, he couches it in the same copious diction that he had used in 3:2: "gift of God's grace, which was given to me." This fullness of expression should help us to feel in turn the fullness of heart from which it stems. "... *given by the working of his power*." Whenever we hear Paul using the word "power" ("*dynamis*"), the thought of the resurrection is almost always in the offing. This was the case in 1:19f. We were to know "what is the tremendous force of his *power* ... in the strength... which he exerted on Christ, as he raised him up from the dead..." And this power which raised Christ from the dead was described in the same place as "the tremendous force *in regard to us* who believe." So the power which raised up Christ from the dead works on and spreads by creating the life of the resurrection in those who have been taken up by faith and baptism into the death and resurrection of Christ. Since this is brought about by faith, that is to say, by the Gospel, Paul can say of the Gospel that it is "the *power* [*dynamis*] of God unto salvation for all who believe, for the Jews first, and then for the Gentiles" (Rom 1:16). Now it becomes clear to us what Paul is aiming at when he says, in a way so astonishing to us, that the service of the Gospel has been conferred upon him as a gift of God's grace, "by the working of his power." He sees that by being called to proclaim the Gospel, he has been drawn into that great movement of the divine energy which raised up Christ from the dead, which makes the message of the resurrection "a divine power unto salvation for all who believe," and which finally leads this salvation towards its fulfillment in preaching has been entrusted to him as a share in the working of the power of God which communicates the life of the resurrection. In face of such a great call, Paul feels himself reduced to very little.

"To me, the least of all the saints, this grace was given, to proclaim to the Gentiles the Gospel of the unfathomable riches of Christ." As the sentence stands, not linked by a conjunction to the foregoing, it gives the impression of a cry of wonder rather than a simple statement. "*To me, the least of all.*" Once more the vocabulary of ordinary speech is not enough for Paul. From a superlative ("the least") he forms a new degree of comparison, as though to say, "To me, less than the least of all the saints." We are reminded of other places where Paul is brought up against the overwhelming greatness of God's grace, and feels his nothingness, his real unworthiness, so deeply that he compares himself to a sort of a miscarriage: "And last of all, as though to one born out of due time, he appeared also to me" (1 Cor 15:8). His past, when he persecuted God's Church, is still present to Paul's mind, even at the height of his activity. And hence he goes on: "Indeed, I am the least of the apostles, not worthy to be called an apostle, because I persecuted the Church of God." But the lower his personal estimate of himself, the higher his appreciation of what the grace of God accomplishes in him: ". . . but by the grace of God I am what I am, and his grace did not prove useless in me, but I have labored more than them all, no, not I, but the grace of God with me" (1 Cor 15:9f.). So, too, in our present text, he stands in his littleness in front of the great grace of his call, which is like new to him, though he is old and grey.

The demonstrative adjective "this," in "*this* grace," should no doubt be dwelled upon and underlined. We should read it as an expression of astonishment in face of the grace of "*proclaiming to the Gentiles the Gospel of the unfathomable riches of Christ.*" Here two loves find expression, his love for the Gentiles and his love for Christ.

"To the Gentiles" comes with the strongest emphasis at the beginning. The verb used for "proclaiming" has still the full ring of the "good tidings," and this Gospel does not merely tell about Christ; no, it actually brings Christ with it and unites men to Christ. But Christ is rich, and he enriches men with what he has, and still more, with what he is, with himself. Paul knows something of these *riches, which Christ is*. He has experienced it, he experiences it continually, not just as others do, but in a uniquely inspired depth of comprehension. Hence he maintained confidently against the Corinthians, who are themselves abundantly endowed with extraordinary spiritual gifts: glory. This is what the Apostle means when he writes that the "I thank God, that I speak more in the language of ecstasy than all of you" (1 Cor 14:18). But he knows that he possesses the other spiritual gifts as well: "If I came to you and spoke only in the language of ecstasy, what good would it be to you, if I did not speak to you with the [charisma] of revelation or knowledge, or in spiritual discourse or in doctrine?" (1 Cor 14:6). These are all gifts which express or suppose the privilege of deep, inspired knowledge, especially the grace of "revelation," which is a sort of penetrating vision of reality. Since that is the way Paul was equipped for his work of preaching, we can appreciate what it means when he calls the riches of Christ "unfathomable." The word means more precisely "beyond reach of our search." No matter what may have been grasped, there is always still more which escapes our grasp. But let us remember always that the main emphasis is clearly laid upon the fact that it is to the *Gentiles* that he can bring these good tidings.

"... and to bring to light how the mystery is realized, which had been hidden from eternity in God, the creator of all." This is not a second task which Paul feels himself called to. The conjunction "and" is explicative, and corresponds more or less to our "that is to say." Hence the plan of salvation is made luminously clear to all by the very fact that the Apostle preaches Christ to the Gentiles, not in any ordinary fashion, but with that grace-laden power which brings about faith, and so union with Christ and salvation. Thus God's plan of salvation is put into effect in the Gentile world.

Now, however, a special note is added, that this plan of salvation had led a hidden existence from eternity, "*in God, the creator of all.*" Paul has a very vivid sense of such pre-temporal elements in the eternal thoughts of God. Did he not, at the very beginning, start to describe the blessings of God by insisting that God has chosen us "before the foundation of the world" (1:4)? And just as he follows God's plan of salvation back to the primal, eternal causes, so likewise he sees it working out in all the coming aeons: God has accomplished the work "in order to make known in the coming aeons the overwhelming riches of his grace" (2:7). He sees the work of salvation inserted, as it were, between two eternities, which really reveal its full significance, because it is the center of both.

"... *in God, the creator of all.*" Commentators have correctly suspected here a *polemical point directed against currents of a Gnostic type*. These spiritual movements divided the world into two parts, a world of thought and a world of sense, into spirit and matter. Hence they came to maintain that the God of creation, who had created matter, was an evil being, whom they contrasted with the good God, the Father of Jesus Christ. The phrase which says that the mystery of our redemption was hidden

" in God the creator of all things " may well be directed against such efforts at dissociating the work of creation from redemption. It can be a warning for us also not to make too sharp a division between body and soul, nature and grace, creation and redemption. We must try to see them in conjunction and do full justice to both.

If our reading of the above passage is correct, we must then allow for the fact that Paul is addressing himself, more than we can check, to a spiritual *milieu* which we can no longer reconstruct except in fragments and by conjecture. And yet we should really know this spiritual background, because it occasionally determines the language of the Apostle, and because it is only there that his words have their proper resonance and make the exact impression which he intended.

It is possible, therefore, that when Paul speaks of aeons, the first readers of the letter understood something more and something different than what we render with the purely temporal concepts of " eternities " or even " ages of history."

" *. . . so that now the manifold wisdom of God should be made known, through the Church, to the powers and authorities in the heavens, in accordance with his eternal purpose, which he has accomplished in Christ Jesus our Lord.*"

We have already encountered the " *powers and authorities* " (1:21). Christ is exalted high above them, and they with all others, are subjected to his Lordship. They will be spoken of again as hostile powers in 6:12—" We have to fight not against flesh and blood, but against the powers . . . against the spiritual beings of wickedness in the heavens." Thus Paul describes, in the language and concepts of his day, something that is always true: There is such a thing as Satan and his world of spirits, who fight in implacable hatred against God and his anointed, Christ, who conquered them on the cross and basically reduced them to impotence. This is Paul's view of these "powers and authorities."

But the recipients of the epistle, in the hinterland of Ephesus, were dominated by other ideas. For them, these "powers and authorities," whether good or evil, were precisely what their name said: "powers and authorities," with whom it was better to keep on good terms. Hence an honor paid to angels, and a cult of powers, which cast about in all directions and put Christ in the shadow, when it did not call him in question altogether. Paul took up the question in the Epistle to the Colossians, and the magnificent texts there about the absolute sovereignty of Christ in creation are due to this heretical effort to depreciate Christ. In the Epistle to the Ephesians interest in these powers and authorities seems to be fading, as in the present text. What good are they, these powers and authorities, from whom misguided Christians expect wisdom and "*gnosis*," insight into the mysteries of the celestial sphere and into the ways that lead to salvation (Col 2:3f. 8)? What good are they, these powers and authorities? They had not the least suspicion of a true plan of salvation, of the mystery of God! Now they must listen to the preaching of the Apostle, and go to school in the Church of Gentiles and Jews united in Christ, the Church which as his "body" and his "fullness" in this world, and which establishes itself wherever the Gospel's message of salvation is proclaimed. There they must look to see, even if it grates on them, what is really "the wisdom of God," and how rich and "manifold" it is.

"*Manifold*" suggests the thought of a wisdom which if

baulked of one way, comes by another and a better one, and hence all the more gloriously to its goal. And so it was in fact: " Since in the wisdom of God [set forth in creation] the world with its wisdom did not know God, it pleased God, through the foolishness of the message [of the cross], to save those who were to believe in it " (1 Cor 1:21). In place of the glory of creation appears the cross, in place of human wisdom comes faith. But this faith unites us to Christ, and makes Christ become for us " the power of God and the wisdom of God " (1 Cor 1:24). Here, no doubt, in our present context, Paul is rather thinking of Christ who is " our peace." The peace of men among themselves, Jews and Gentiles one body in Christ, and in this body of Christ the fullness of divine life: that is how the powers and authorities—who being spiritual powers do not stop at externals— see the Church of Christ, and in it God's " manifold wisdom."

"*In Christ Jesus, our Lord.*" How should Paul be able even to mention him without adding something about what he means for us? Hence here he says: " in whom we have been given full assurance and free access, in confident faith in him." The Church, as the body of Christ, is from now on *the* place where God is near. This is indicated by the words " free access." And since we approach Christ endowed with his holiness and relying only upon him, boundless confidence is *the* Christian attitude— with regard to God, and thereby with regard to this world and this life, where " for those who love God, all things work for good " necessarily (Rom 8:28), and suffering is only the passage to glory (2 Cor 1:7; Acts 14:22).

Paul now applies all this to his readers and to his own situation as prisoner. " Wherefore I pray not to lose heart on account of my tribulations in your behalf; for they are indeed a source of pride for you." All that is wanting is that he should add, as in the Epistle to the Colossians, " Now I rejoice at my sufferings for you . . ." (Col 1:24).

Looking back on this last section, we may make the following observation. From 2:1 on, Paul has been celebrating " the mystery of Christ," which ultimately is Christ himself. One feels, as it were, the joy of his heart at the grandeur of this mystery and at the fact that he was allowed to proclaim it: and no wonder, since the riches of Christ are unfathomable. " Christ in you, the hope of glory " was the way he had summed up this mystery in Col 1:27. But if we are really to do justice to Paul, we must not overlook the fact that for him the mystery is normally seen from one very special side, which is *Christ as redeemer of the heathens also*. This is the side of the redemptive work for which Paul, so to speak, gives chapter and verse. He can scarcely grasp it. It fills him with astonishment and immense joy. Some explanation is needed of this jubilation at something which we later arrivals take for granted: the equal rights of the Gentiles along with the chosen people. To show what Paul himself may have once felt about it, we may take perhaps a saying of the Rabbi Akiba. He was one of the noblest figures of early rabbinism (he died as a martyr about A.D. 135, with the precept of charity from Deut 6 on his lips). When expounding upon the text of the Canticle of Canticles where we find the words " My well-beloved," his comment was as follows: " When the nations of the earth hear these words, they will say to the Israelites: We wish to come with you, we wish to seek for him along with you. But the Israelites will answer them: You have no share along with us. My well-beloved belongs to me and I to him."

Paul, as a Jew, must have had the same feeling. What a distance he must have travelled, when the conferring of the same rights upon the Gentiles now gives him *the* great joy of his heart. A change has come about which is no less than miraculous. When God gave his chosen instrument his call to the apostolate of the Gentiles, he must at the same time have put an overwhelming love into Paul's heart. The jubilant thanksgiving, which must appear so incomprehensible to us, shows us the extent of this love. It is, as it were, an "incarnation" of the love of God itself for the Gentiles, or rather, it can only be Jesus Christ himself who loves these Gentiles in his instrument, Paul. He writes in one place: "God is my witness, how deeply I long for you all, *en splanchois Christi Jesu*" (Phil 1:8). We can only translate the Greek by "in the heart of Jesus," or, abandoning the metaphor, "in the love of Christ Jesus." Our text from the Epistle to the Ephesians has therefore been rightly adopted into the liturgy of the Church as the epistle for the feast of the Sacred Heart. We for our part, however, should be fully aware of the fact that here is a grace for which we must make efforts, and must cherish carefully, as soon as it awakens timidly in our hearts: love of the pagan world, which as yet knows nothing of the riches of Christ. Even if this love sprang only from a deep gratitude for what we possess!

## The Apostle's Prayer in Behalf of the Faithful for Fullness of Knowledge (3:14-19)

With the solemn "for the sake of which," Paul takes up once more the formula which marked the transition to 3:1. There he had already intended to speak of his prayer for knowledge in the faithful. But then came the long interruption dealing with his own share in the "mystery of Christ" in the Gentile world. The greater the matter which Paul has expounded in the preceding verses, the deeper does he feel that the presentation of the case alone does not suffice. Something more than the intellect must be appealed to here. The necessary reaction to this divine mystery can be brought about only by the Spirit of God and the grace of God. Hence the Apostle prays. And he goes so straight into his prayer that one gets the impression that Paul sees his vocation in this prayerful mediation, as much as in his preaching.

*[14] Wherefore I bend my knees to the Father [15] from whom all fatherhood in heaven and on earth has its name. [16] May he grant you, according to the riches of his glory, to be strengthened in power through his Spirit in the inward man, [17] that Christ may dwell through faith in your hearts, and that you may be firmly rooted and grounded in love, [18] so that you may be capable of grasping, with all the saints, what is the breadth and length and height and depth, [19] and know the love of Christ which surpasses all knowledge, that you may be filled unto the whole fullness of God.*

He begins solemnly: "*Wherefore I bend my knees . . .*" To kneel is unusual for Paul and for every Jew, because the Israelite stood to pray to his God. It must, therefore, be more than the intention of praying that makes Paul sink down upon his knees, spiritually, here.

### The Father of All "Fatherhood" (3:14–15)

Paul turns to the *"Father, from whom all fatherhood in heaven and on earth has its name."* It is ultimately quite correct that God is here understood as the first cause of all other fatherhood, as *the* Father in the absolute sense. But the Greek word, taken over from the Old Testament, means strictly speaking " a fathering," not in the abstract sense of " being a father," but in the concrete sense of a number of people who all go back to the same ancestor. It is a " paternity " understood somewhat like a fraternity. Hence "fatherhood" here means family, clan, or people—in a word, every natural social formation of mankind. Something similar is assumed to be true of the spirit world with its various orders of beings. Indeed, these families or " paternities " among the spirits " in heaven " are named here in the first place, once more no doubt with a side-glance at the false cult of angels, which threatened the purity of the faith of the readers. God is the Father from whom even those heavenly families derive.

But the " paternities " on earth, too, peoples and nations, all have the one Father in God, and not only the chosen people. And God has proved himself in truth to be the Father of the " peoples " by calling the " peoples "—the Jewish term for the pagans—to salvation in Jesus Christ. This is implicit in the fact that Paul turns to pray to the Father from whom all paternity in heaven and earth " has its name," that is, once more in Semitic terms, has its natural existence.

Finally, God is named as creator again, as already in 3:9. No one should let himself be deceived into finding fault with the creator of the world and his work of creation. It is the same God who created this world and who redeems it in Jesus Christ.

## The Presuppositions for Perfect Knowledge (3:16–17)

" May [God] grant you, according to the riches of his glory . . ." Once more we have, as in 1:17, this confident appeal to God's glory. As we saw there, it is an appeal to the riches of God, which in its abundance seeks to impart itself. And it is likewise an appeal to the God who "sanctifies his name," precisely by stooping to help and enrich his people, which then in turn glorifies him for it in thankfulness.

"... *to be strengthened with power through the Spirit in the inward man*" (more precisely, unto the inward man). What is this "inward man"? We find the word in 2 Cor 4:16 in express contrast to the "outward man": "And even if the outward man is destroyed [in the service of the Gospel], yet the inward man is renewed from day to day." It is the man who has been created anew in baptism,[15] the "man in Christ" who is described so beautifully in 1 Pet 3:4 as "the hidden man of the heart." He is the work of the Spirit, and so it is understandable that the desired "strengthening of the inward man" can only take place "through the Spirit."

But why the precision "*unto* the inward man"? This sounds as though the "inner man" represented a measure of ripeness, the "full stature" of Christ (4:13), in so far as each individual is to realize it in turn. It is the divinely willed goal of the "new man," not as he has been fundamentally created in baptism, but of the "new man" who is yet to be put on "in true righteousness and holiness."

"... *that Christ may dwell through faith in your hearts*." The ancients knew what "to dwell" means. And the men of today have to a great extent learned it again, namely, that it is something more than "to have housing." To be housed means to pass one's life in some place that offers shelter. But one can only dwell, in the sense of being at home, in surroundings which are the proper setting for one's life. And one really dwells somewhere, one feel's all the more at home, the more every detail of one's surroundings, through one's work, or at least by personal choice, is the expression of the personality living there. Now, wherever Christ takes up his abode, he brings all the essentials with him and gives the inward man the form of Christ. But this basic and essential conformity to Christ must still be accomplished, to a great extent, by the host, though of course in the Spirit, and by the power of the divine guest. Such a consideration helps us to see more vividly that there can be degrees of " dwelling," and that it can reach a stage of perfection, which is no doubt intended here.

" . . . *firmly rooted and grounded in love* . . ." The two expressions, and the tense which indicates something definitive (the perfect), make us think once more of a degree of perfection which is the object of Paul's prayer. He asks for a perfect stability in love, in love at all costs and all along the line, in love which is the foundation and ground of one's whole life, where it stands, whence it draws nourishment. The two metaphors, one taken from gardening, the other from architecture, do not fit well together, but Paul uses both of them: the nourishing soil of the roots, and the unshakeable foundations.

## Perfect Knowledge (3:18-19)

The Apostle has enumerated three things which have an intrinsic connection with each other: growing strong in the Spirit, the indwelling of Christ, the perfection of love. These are objects of prayer, not for their own sake, but for the sake of what Paul is most closely concerned with: "*that you may be capable of grasping, with all the saints.*" Thus the real object of his prayer is *knowledge*.

Is that not a sort of concession to his readers, who prize knowledge, *gnosis,* above everything else? It may indeed be a concession, but such are the paths along which revelation comes and along which it leads its bearers. New questions, difficulties that arise, and even heresies, lead to new efforts to penetrate and master the contents of revelation, so that it can meet all justifiable demands, and in doing so itself grow and expand—as long as the epoch of revelation still lasts.

"*. . . with all the saints . . .*" It is therefore a matter of knowledge, to which it is essential that it be shared with others, indeed with all who have been called—" the saints." It is not therefore a matter of the jealous preservation of secret doctrines, which seem all the more precious the smaller the circle of those who are initiated into them. Here it is a matter of knowledge which on principle is forbidden to no one, and is accessible to every single Christian (Col 1:28). In the last resort, it is meant to be transformed into a jubilant chant on the lips of all the redeemed, into a joy which is multiplied as it is shared.

### THE OBJECT OF KNOWLEDGE (3:18b–19a)

The object of this knowledge is now indicated in two ways. The first is enigmatic for us. It is " the breadth and length and height and depth," but of what is not said. And then comes, in the closest possible connection with this " grasp " of the dimensions in question: " and to know the love of Christ which surpasses all knowledge."

"*The breadth and length and height and depth.*" What is it, that it is so necessary to know, and which is placed in such close conjunction with the knowledge of the love of Christ, with which, therefore, presumably it is in continuity? Commentators sometimes have simply taken the two objects of knowledge to be really the same, and referred the dimensions to the love of Christ. But that is to do violence to the text, which makes a clear distinction between the dimensions and the love. The universe has been suggested, but knowledge of the universe may have had some significance in the Gnostic view of salvation, for Christians it had none. Does it perhaps mean the all-embracing character of the plan of salvation? But then why is it not stated? Perhaps because it is obvious? All the same, we have the feeling that this expression was familiar to the writer and his readers, and no less clear than " the love of Christ " which comes immediately after. We have to distinguish between *what* Paul means, and the imagery in which he clothes his thought. In view of all that has been said hitherto, the only thing that Paul can *mean* is the " mystery of Christ," considered under the particular aspect which has been so predominant in the whole section (2:1ff.): not Christ simply and solely, but *Christ for the Gentiles*.

Even if the origin of the dimensions-formula remains obscure, we still have the important fact that Paul must have meant thereby all that he wrote about the reconciliation of Gentiles and Jews in one body of Christ. It would be, therefore, the comprehensiveness of this work of redemption which was voiced in this formula. And, in fact, has not this reconciliation of the heathen world an immeasureable " breadth," since it embraces the whole world of the nations? Has it not a " length " that stretches back into eternity, where this plan had been hidden by God (3:9)? Has it not a bottomless " depth," of distance and enstrangement from God, from which it rescues this humanity (2:1. 2. 11. 12)? Has it not its " height," for which it prepares this world of the nations? " High above all powers and authorities," where Christ is enthroned, the Lord of the world, the head of the Church (1:20-22)?

Finally, if we are to think here of Christ's work of unification, such as the Lord accomplished on the cross, then we can understand why the Apostle speaks in such immediate connection with it of the love of Christ. For this "love of Christ" appears elsewhere too in the epistle as the love which dedicates itself for us and for the Church (5:2. 25).

Hence to grasp the "mystery of Christ" in all its grandeur is, we may say, to know the love of Christ. There, 3:18, the verb was "grasp," "seize," "master," in the sense of making something one's inward acquisition. Here, 3:19, the verb is "to know." But, as we have seen, this word "know" meant much more to the Semite than it does to us! For him, knowledge does not take place so much in that thin, superficial level of our being which we call the intellect. In the language of sacred Scripture, knowledge is something which involves the whole man and lays claim to him totally.

Now, however, it is added that this love of Christ "surpasses all knowledge." And yet the Apostle prays that we should know it. That can only mean that the love of Christ is only known when in the effort to grasp it we become aware of the fact that it is unfathomable and beyond all comprehension. It is an object of ever new wonder, which one will never be done with, even through the length of an eternity with God.

### The effects of this knowledge (3:19b)

This knowledge of the love of Christ is to lead to their being "*filled unto the whole fullness of God.*" Our text is rounded off with a thought of bewildering magnitude. The "fullness of

God," which dwells in Christ, is to enter into us and to "fill" us, which is to come about when the love of Christ dawns on us. Who can follow this? In order to make these words to some extent understandable, commentators have tried to take the fullness of God as meaning the "full stature of Christ" (4:13), in so far as it is *God* who lays down for it a certain measure of achievement. But would Paul call this the "whole fullness of God"? The thought of the full mature stature of Christ may play a part in the expression, but if so, it indicates precisely that final stage where the whole fullness of God, which dwells in Christ, prevails fully, as the fullness of his Church (1:23). What can that mean for each individual?

It means something like this. When we really become aware of these two things, the span of Christ's work of salvation which embraces the world and eternity, and the love of Christ which is its innermost driving force, then the fullness of God is disclosed to us, *therein*.

Do we not think spontaneously of John? "He who sees me, sees also the Father" (14:9)? The Word made man is *the* revelation of the Father, and this Father reveals himself in Christ as love. To have a deep, intimate knowledge of this personal love of God for us, and to be aware of it because it is present in us through the indwelling of Christ—this is "to be filled with the whole fullness of God." But when Paul says more precisely, "unto the whole fullness of God," we may take it that once more the urge towards a perfect final stage is being voiced. But then what does it mean to grow and ripen, if this fullness already dwells concretely in Christ the bearer of the fullness of God, and through him in us? The point can only be that this fullness now penetrates our very consciousness ever more deeply and vividly, and that it manifests itself in a life filled with God.

All the same, there is much in this section which remains obscure. In these last verses, Paul soars off on a lofty flight which leaves us far, far behind, bewildered and astonished, and yet filled with a deep joy, and believing confidently in what we do not understand. We must not forget that the possessor of the extraordinary gifts of the Spirit is speaking here. He was granted them in superabundant measure in view of the preaching of the message of salvation. It is said that charismas are anticipations of the last days. Should we then be surprised if Paul seems to speak of the present, and yet describes at the same time the final state towards which this present is to move? He is speaking of what he himself possesses, otherwise he would include himself in his prayer. He desires his followers to reach the place whither he already has come on the wings of the Spirit.

### To God Be the Glory (3:20–21)

*[20]But to him who has the power to accomplish all things superabundantly, immeasurably more than we can ask for or imagine, according to the power which is at work in us, [21]to him be glory in the Church and in Christ Jesus through all the generations of the aeon of the aeons. Amen.*

It was with a hymn of praise and thanksgiving that this first part of the epistle began. It ends, too, with a solemn utterance in praise of God. With a twofold hyperbole, Paul emphasizes God's power to hear our prayers, which is infinitely beyond all we can think of or ask for. Paul does this partly because he is himself overwhelmed by what he hopes for in behalf of his faithful, and partly also perhaps because he is conscious of a sort of contradiction in what went before. For he had asked for knowledge for them which does not and cannot exist, namely, to know something that "surpasses all knowledge," and likewise a knowledge which exhausts, as it were, for us " the whole fullness of God." It is understandable that he should see and describe the power to hear prayer, on which he counts, as no less boundless.

". . . *according to the power, which is at work in us.*" This could be read as follows: " beyond all that we can conceive by virtue of the power which we *experienced* at work in us." But is not this interpretation too bold? Is it not perhaps still the charismatic, Paul, who is speaking, though in the plural " we," while thinking precisely of himself and his own experience? However, more probably " according to the power " is to be referred to God, who " can accomplish everything superabundantly," through the power which is already at work in us.

This power (*dynamis*) was already mentioned (3:16), and we reminded ourselves that Paul mostly understands *dynamis* as the life of the resurrection effected by the Spirit. In 1:19 it was the power of God which had raised up Christ, and which Paul there called " the power of God with regard to us believers." This would then be the power which is said to be at work in us here. And just as it is said in 2:7 that God has raised us up together with Christ, " thus to make known to the coming aeons the riches of his grace with regard to us," so too here the work of his " power " appears as the reason for God's eternal glory: " To him be the glory . . . through all generations of the aeon of the aeons. Amen."

This glory is to be given him " in the Church," and " in Christ Jesus." This undoubtedly means in the Church, which is " in Christ Jesus " and which is true to its " being in Christ." The Church has to be, for all the generations to come, the shining glory of God in this world, the banner raised on high for the world of the nations through all the days of history. What a concept of the Church, and what a responsibility for all its members! Thus the transition is effected to the second portion of the epistle, which is the part of it that gives exhortations on practical matters.

# LIVING THE TRUTH (4:1—6:22)

In accordance with the Pauline way of constructing a letter, the exhortatory portion now follows, after the doctrinal part. Paul manages to speak here of all and everything, exhorting to one thing, warning against another: against lies, impurity, anger, avarice, and "all the works of darkness." These rules hold for all. Then he turns to the various states of life, with a word of exhortation for husband and wife, parents and children, slaves and masters. The Apostle's address takes up many subjects, as varied as only the Christian way of life can be, but each of the items is treated relatively briefly.

## Preserving the Unity of the Spirit (4:1-6)

It is highly significant that Paul anticipates one element of this Christian moral doctrine, to put it in the very first place and to expound it fully. It must therefore be something in moral matters which he has at heart beyond all else. It is the unity of the members in the body of Christ, the unity of the Church in love and peace. These quite general disquisitions give us no reason at all to think that there was any particular danger threatening Church unity in those regions of the East which would give this subject special importance. No, clearly for Paul in the Epistles of the Captivity, in his whole thinking of the faith, and in all his apostolic cares, unity is his *great interest,* and it therefore forces its way to the front. It is all the more important, therefore, that we should yield to the insistence of the Apostle, and make his interest our own.

### *The Presuppositions:*
### *Humility and Patient Love (4:1-3)*

*¹I urge you, therefore, I, the prisoner in the Lord, to let your life be worthy of the call by which you were called, ²in all humility and meekness, with patience bearing with one another in love, ³in order to preserve zealously the unity of the Spirit in the bond of peace.*

" . . . *therefore.*" This " so now " is once more of fundamental importance, because it effects the union between dogma and life, between faith and action. For it implies nothing less than that Christian life, as Paul is going to describe it, is but a natural consequence of the doctrine developed in the first part. A way of life should follow at once from all that has been said about the blessings of God's grace, the mystery of Christ and the innermost, God-given being of the Christian. Christian existence is life wrought by God, and life is impelled to "live itself out." Christian reality is a force, and this force strives to go into action. Christian reality is a call from God, and this call demands an answer which is worthy of the call.

"*I urge you.*" There is, unfortunately, no word in English which does justice to the full force of this Pauline "*parakaleo.*" This verb means "to exhort," but also to entreat, summon, conjure, and also to console. Behind this word, as the Apostle uses it, there is the urgent force of his supreme authority, but also anxiety, love, understanding—in a word, the whole heart of Paul.

And he wishes to speak to the hearts of the faithful. Hence the "*I, the prisoner in the Lord.*" The fetters of the Apostle, the powerlessness of the captive, the prison garb in which he writes, should throw open their hearts and arouse them to readiness—even for sacrifice. For they know that Paul bears his chains because of his mission to the Gentiles, that is, on account of them.

"*. . . to let your life be worthy of the call by which you were* *called."* This call has the nature of an obligation by reason of God who calls, and by reason of the goal to which he calls. For Paul, especially in this epistle, " call " and " hope " always go together (see 1:18; 4:4). Hence he summons his readers to live up to the hope upon which Christian life is based and to which Christian life tends, the magnificent hope which is founded upon the election by the Father (1:4) and upon the redemptive work of the Son (1:7), and which is guaranteed by the Holy Spirit in our hearts (1:14).

What does a life " worthy of the call " consist of, according to Paul? It comprises all that follows, but, as we can see, first and foremost humility, meekness, patience and pardon, mutual forbearance for the sake of a high goal, and peace " *to preserve the unity of the Spirit.*" After all that has been said about the Church as the body of Christ, this means maintaining the unity which has been brought about by the Holy Spirit in person in the one body of Christ. We are told to " maintain" it. It is already there, as the work of the Spirit. The Christian finds it there in advance, and sees himself faced with the task of never disturbing this permanent divine action, and of making every effort to preserve the work of God.

The way to do this is described by Paul as a life literally " accompanied by," and therefore in fact guided by " all humility and meekness." " All " is what he says, and so means not humility now and then, occasionally, at discretion, when it suits, but humility all along the line, in all its forms, in all its manifestations, humility which flows from the innermost attitude of the soul and its basic disposition.

What does *humility* mean? The Greek word could be rendered in English quite exactly as " lowly mindedness " (compare " high-minded "—though of course " low-minded " would not do here!)

It is the attitude of a man who is bent on what is lowly, what is small and unremarkable, what is unjustly despised and avoided by others. His mind is set on this, and hence his first wish is to serve. The humble man is therefore "serviceable," in the sense of ready to serve, as the word was used of the angels by Milton.

Humility, then, is the deliberate renunciation of grandeur and importance in the eyes of men, of honors, respect, importance, and authority. It also includes the opposite urge, the desire to be out of the limelight and to remain unnoticed. But that is the death of the natural self, which ever since the fall of our first parents, if left to itself, always strives for superiority. The allurement of that "You shall be like God" is in our blood ever since Adam. What humility means, and how the "mind of Jesus Christ" is its great motive and exemplar, can be read in the Epistle to the Philippians (2:5-8). Being like to God did not weigh with Christ. He emptied himself to the form of a servant and the death of the cross. That was indeed a plunge into the depths!

Next to humility, and closely linked to it, comes *meekness*. It is that gentleness which can renounce all violence and harshness in the pursuit of success, which does not hit back when it receives a blow, which knows how to give way in all the trifling conflicts of human life, because it knows of something better than self-assertion. It is a meekness such as is called blessed by the Lord (Mt 5:5), and which he claimed for himself, along with humility, as characteristic of his nature (Mt 11:29).

"... *to preserve zealously the unity of the Spirit in the bond of peace.*" In the present context, peace suggests first of all the elimination of strife and discord, and yet it also evokes something of the amplitude of meaning in "peace" when used by Paul: the peace of God, who is "the God of peace" (Rom 15:33), in

Christ, who is himself " our peace " (Eph 2:14-17), through the
Holy Spirit of God, among whose " fruits " peace is numbered
(Gal 5:22). Thus in Paul, " peace " is a divine gift, which makes
us think of Father, Son, and Holy Spirit. And when Paul *exhorts*
to peace, we have here once more the authentically Pauline
merging of God's action and man's deed.


*The Reasons for It (4:4-6)*

*⁴One body and one spirit, as you were also called to the one hope
of your calling. ⁵One Lord, one faith, one baptism. ⁶One God
and Father of all [who is] over all and [works] through all and
[dwells] in all.*


The reasons why we should be zealous for the unity of the Spirit
are given here by Paul in a series of stirring thoughts which rise
to a powerfully eloquent climax in a profusion which is almost
oppressive. In three groups of three motives, Paul mounts from
the unity of the body in the Spirit, by the unity of the *Kyrios,*
to the unity of God.

This *Body of Christ,* which is the Church, is well known to us
by now. It is named here first, even before the Spirit, because
Paul is primarily concerned here with its maintenance, and also
perhaps because the thought of a living organism makes us feel
most palpably the contradiction of allowing anything to affect
this body which might wound, rend, or kill it.

" . . . *one Spirit.*" He is like the soul of this body, he is the
real creator of it as a living being, he binds it together, since he
is the source of life and the constructive principle in this abode of
God (2:22). The Spirit is a person, whom we should take care

not to " grieve " (4:30). He is the Spirit who is the surety and guarantee of our hope, " the pledge of our inheritance " (1:14). That is perhaps the reason why Paul does not simply continue with " one hope," but links this hope closely to the Holy Spirit: " for you have also been called to the one hope of your calling." Not to keep the unity of the Spirit means therefore to sin against the reality in which the Christian is allowed to live, against one body, against one Spirit, and against the great hope.

" *One Lord.*" This is the jubilant confession of the First Christians; it is what made them Christians. Behind it lies what Paul had written in the Epistle to the Philippians: " Wherefore God has given him the name which is above all names. . . , so that every tongue may confess. . . : Jesus Christ is the Lord " (2:9-11). And he is *our* Lord, he is the head of which we have become the members through the " one faith "—which is "God's gift" (2:8)—and the " one baptism," in which we have been given the divine seal of the Holy Spirit (1:13), and have entered into the death and resurrection of Christ (2:5. 6), truly baptized together into one body (1 Cor 12:13), and become " one person " (Gal 3:28) in Christ Jesus, all of us. We can well believe that to disregard such a oneness, to offend against it, is nothing short of ceasing to believe in the " one Lord " and the " one baptism."

The last in the ascending order, the first in the order of causes, is *the Father*. He does not appear here linked up in a triad, like "the one Lord" and "the one Spirit." He stands alone, as it were, in lonely majesty and supremacy. The triple note, which is not missing even her, only divides up his modes of action. Literally, the text reads: " One God and Father of all, the one over all and through all and in all." The Greek text does not help us to decide whether " all " means everything or " everyone." But since Paul is treating of the unity of the faithful, we should, no doubt, rather incline to the translation " everyone."

" *One God* " here means less a sort of external contrast to other gods than the intrinsic quality, the unifying force, which this oneness of God exerts. But now the name of Father is added at once. Thereby the unifying principle of the oneness of God receives the warm personal note of love, and is seen as the relation of the one Father to his many children. And then, it is said of this loving Father of all—when we fill in what is understood in the original text—that he reigns " over all," ruling them, watching over them, caring for them. He works " through all ": none of his children lives for himself, each of them is somehow or other in the service of his fatherly love and is to be its instrument. And finally, he dwells " in all." Our love meets him in our brothers and finds its way back to him, just as it has come forth from him. " For the love of God is poured forth into our hearts by the Holy Spirit " (Rom 5:5).

Here, then, is the deepest motivation of the effort to maintain the unity of the Spirit. It is the primary and basic motive, which includes all that has gone before. For God's indwelling " in all " is accomplished now in Christ, the " one Lord," and through the one Holy Spirit.

## Christ Building Up His Body (4:7-16)

The train of thought now leads on to a task which goes beyond the mere " preservation " of the unity of the Spirit. We come now to the active contribution which every member of the body of Christ is called to make to its growth and expansion, by virtue of what he receives from Christ.

## Christ the Giver of All Gifts of Grace (4:7–12)

### FOR THIS HAS HE ENTERED ON HIS LORDSHIP ON HIGH (4:7-10)

*⁷But grace was given to each one of us according to the measure of the gift of Christ. ⁸Hence Scripture says: "Ascending on high, he brought captives with him, he gave gifts to men." ⁹Now, what else can be implied by the words " he ascended," except that he also descended into the lower parts of the earth? ¹⁰He who descended is the very one who ascended above all the heavens, to fill all.*

Ostensibly, Paul here gives the Scripture proof for the truth that Christ is really the giver of heavenly grace. But it is only apparently so, because the text of Scripture which he adduces is not correctly given, and the deduction which he makes from it is not logically valid. It will be perhaps helpful to take seriously this example of the " incarnation " of God's word. For we should not apply to Paul the rules of today's " Scripture proofs." Paul had been in the school of the rabbis. It is no wonder, then, that their method of exploiting texts of Scripture influenced the biblical thinking of the Apostle. In the original text of the Psalm which he quotes, the very point which Paul wishes to make is missing. We read in the original, not " he gave gifts to men," but the opposite: " He has accepted gifts among men," or perhaps: " He has accepted men as gifts." Paul apparently does not keep to the strict text of Scripture, but follows a rabbinical interpretation, which applied this verse of the Psalm to Moses, as he went up to Sinai to receive the Law and bring it to men as a gift. We have, therefore, an ancient interpretation, which we can still show to have existed, according to which he who "ascended" on high "gave gifts to men."

In the following, Paul tries to demonstrate that the only one who can have "ascended" to heaven is Jesus Christ, who descended to this earth from heaven. But an "ascent" presupposes a "descent" only if one takes it for granted that the text speaks of the redeemer, who has gone up to heaven. Is not this begging the question, supposing what has to be proved? True, but we may not apply our rules of logic where we are dealing with the way the rabbis played with a text of Scripture. How far such considerations really tried to offer a "proof" in our sense remains highly doubtful. A contemporary of Paul, coming from the schools where he had received his formation, would probably not have had the least objection. Paul remains, even as the instrument of the Spirit of inspiration, a man of his own time, a "scribe" or "doctor of the law," not with regard to *what* he has to teach, but still to a great extent in his manner of propounding it.

The ascent is described as going "above all the heavens" in order to "*fill all*." One of the main interests of the epistle, in common with the Epistle to the Colossians, is to insist upon the exclusive supremacy of Christ, not only in the Church and the plan of salvation, but in the whole realm of creation. Hence Paul emphasizes once more this "above all the heavens," a piece of imagery to throw light, as it were, on how Christ can now really "fill the universe." We are reminded of 1:10, and in this context, still more of 1:21f., where Paul described the exhaltation of Christ so exuberantly and then went on: "He has placed all things beneath his feet," to end at last with the thought: "and he gave him as head over all the Church."

These two thoughts, apparently so different—the universal

sovereignty of Christ over the whole creation, and his activity in giving grace, as head of his Church—these two lines of thought come so close together in the mind of Paul that they evoke and penetrate one another. The conjunction of the two concepts is to be explained as follows: for Paul, the sovereignty of Christ over the universe only becomes in reality the filling of this universe, by the fact that Christ fills the Church. To begin with, the exaltation of Christ is only in the nature of a claim to sovereignty. This claim is put into effect originally in the restricted space of the Church. The Church is the "fullness of Christ" (1:23), but in this Church, and through it, and finally by being this Church, the fullness of Christ is to expand and fill the totality of creation. That is the end, the completion of his kingship, a sovereignty unrestricted and acclaimed with joy. That is the kingdom, of which the Scripture says: "When all things have been at last subjected to him, then the Son, too, will submit himself to him who has subjected all things to him, so that God may be all in all" (1 Cor 15:28). That is the Kingdom for whose coming we pray in the Our Father.

This gives us an imposing view of the cosmic, all-embracing destiny of our Church. But does it really embrace the universe, and not just the "world" of humanity, to which the biblical picture of the world would seem to limit it? The restriction is *possible*. But today man is penetrating into the depths of the atom. His science is advancing into distances which are reckoned by billions of light years. Man is becoming a giant who can reach out beyond our planets, not merely in his knowledge, but in his physical activity, literally to the stars. In such an age, of which we as yet know only the first light of dawn, we may at least guess what is the possible destiny of a humanity which is called to be "Church." For this humanity of the last times will in the end bring all things with it, from the atoms to the stars, and place them under the lordship of God, where " God is all in all."

That could very probably be what Paul means to say, unwittingly, to us men of the atomic age when he unites *Christ the Lord of the universe* so intimately in his thought with *Christ the head* and fullness of his Church.

## FOR THE BUILDING UP OF HIS BODY, HE GRANTS OFFICE BEARERS AND BEARERS OF GRACE (4:11-13)

After the brackets of 4:8-10, the main line of thought in 4:7 is taken up again, and now the abundant gifts are enumerated:

*¹¹He gave some as apostles, others as prophets, others as evangelists, others as pastors and teachers, to make ready the saints for the work of service, ¹²for the building-up of the body of Christ, ¹³till we all reach the unity of faith and of knowledge of the Son of God, the mature manhood, the measure of the stature of the fullness of Christ.*

Here two things are noticeable. First, it is not the various graces, as one would expect from 4:7, which appear as gifts, but *bearers of grace*: apostles, inspired speakers ( = " prophets "), missionaries ( = " evangelists "), pastors and teachers—as if the whole man were nothing but his office, and thereby a gift of grace. And then, after " to each one of us " (4:7), one would expect that Paul would speak of *all the members* of the body of Christ. But now the only ones who appear are those whom we call the authorities in the Church. *They* are primarily the " gifts " of the exalted Christ. Primarily, indeed, but then they bring all the others in their train. For these fundamental ministries have been bestowed upon the Church, in order to prepare all the saints " for the work of service, for the building-up of the body of Christ." So we have two things: a clear distinction between those who hold *office and dignities* in the Church—either by official rank or by extraordinary gifts of grace—and those for whose sake office and gift of grace have been bestowed, the " listening " Church, the great mass of the " saints."

However, the individual as such is not the end and object of this ministry: each one is now to do his part of the constructive work on the body of Christ. Office and ministry are present in the Church in order to enable the " other ranks " to do their work. The authorities equip the full member of Christ " for the work of service," and therefore for action, and this action is always the work of building-up. All growth in grace, in the carrying of the cross, in work and prayer, means to build; every effort after " perfection " is a building-up, and should be viewed as such, with regard to the whole. Every transformation of one's surroundings is a building-up. In how many perspectives, then, can all the elements of this life of man be seen!

"... *till we all reach the unity of faith and of knowledge of the Son of God."* This poses all sorts of questions: 1) Who are meant by the words " we all "? If it is all of us who believe, then Paul would not be thinking of expansion. But does " we all " mean those believers and those who are meant to be such? 2) What is meant by the " unity of faith " and of the " knowledge of the Son of God," which is given as the final stage aimed at (" till ")? With the " unity of faith " the " perfect man," the " measure of the stature of the fullness of Christ," is to be attained. And, as is explained in 4:14, the consequences of this should in turn be manly steadfastness in the midst of a world full of temptations. This, of course, has nothing to do with an outward growth of the Church. Steadfastness can only be the consequence of a deepened life of faith. This, then, is what must have been meant by the " unity of faith," which constitutes the " ripe manhood " and the " measure of the stature of the fullness of Christ."

But why does Paul call this deep faith " the unity of faith and of the knowledge of the Son of God "? We are reminded of the " unity of the Spirit," the preservation of which was so earnestly inculcated in the hearts of the readers, at the beginning of the chapter (4:3). Hence the " unity of faith " would not mean the same faith, but the fellowship of the faithful, as it grows together even more firmly, and is all the more intimate, the deeper the common faith, the more lively the common knowledge. After all, the " knowledge of the Son of God " is brought out here with particular emphasis! True knowledge of the Son of God means, in fact, that we know ourselves as " sons in the Son." It means becoming aware of our common sonship as children of God, and thus knowing how deep are the bonds of the brotherhood which unites us all in Christ. We who are many, we are all " one person in Christ Jesus " (Gal 3:28).

Baptism has indeed already made us " one person," but not yet precisely " the full-grown man," not yet the " fullness " which Christ desires to develop in us. Thus the two things correspond. The " unity of faith " is " being one person " in a deepened faith. The " perfect man " is not the perfection of the individual, but the full growth of the whole. Finally, the " measure of the stature of the fullness of Christ " is none other than the Church, which Church pervades and governs through and through.

## The Further Object of the Gifts of Grace (4:14–15)

### CONSTANCY AMID ALL STORMS (4:14)

*... ¹⁴so that we be no longer children, a plaything of the waves and tossed about by every wind of doctrine, victims of the cheating of men, in the midst of a cunning bent on treacherous deceit ...*

When we are really members of a mature Church, united by faith and loving knowledge, truly penetrated by the fullness of Christ (with a knowledge that genuinely fills us), then we have found the solid ground on which we can stand firm and hold fast immovably in the midst of a world which is pulled this way and that by error. Then we are well-settled adults, no longer like restless children, letting ourselves go foolishly and unsuspectingly to every new stream of thought.

Paul piles up the metaphors here to describe the pitiful abandonment of a Christianity which is still immature and not yet firmly anchored in the life of fellowship. Every gust of a new wind of doctrine brings the insecure faith into danger. No doubt, Paul is here envisaging primarily what he designates in the Epistle to the Colossians as " philosophy and idle deceit, in the line of human traditions, looking to the natural forces of the world and not to Christ " (Col 2:8). These were currents of thought which presented themselves in manifold forms, in changing disguises, pressing in upon the Church to win its members by force or flattery, but in any case trying to " carry them along with them " (Col 2:8).

To ward off such onslaughts, the Christian needs ballast and good anchorage, he needs " to be rooted in Christ and built in him, growing constantly stronger in the faith . . . and overflowing with thankfulness," as Paul says in the same place in the Epistle to the Colossians, where he gives a warning against such worldly wisdom and human doctrines (2:7).

But Paul paints in even darker colors *the spiritual atmosphere* in which the Christian has to live. It is characterized as " cheating." Strictly speaking, the word means " dice-playing "; it could also stand for gambling, where all that is precious may be staked and sacrificed thoughtlessly. The meaning here is more probably " cheating," since Paul goes on to speak at once of cunning and seduction. It is well to note here the two aspects of cheating: gambling and falsehood. Such a way of life is a gamble, and he at least who is behind it is bent on deceit.

On top of this comes " cunning." By its derivation, the Greek word would mean the lack of scruples, which is ready for anything. But the usage of the word restricts its meaning to " cunning " or " craftiness." This craftiness aims at practicing deceit in a treacherous and underground fashion, taking advantage of man's simple love of truth.

This description is sinister. It hints at the spirit, " the father of lies." It is amid such dangers from all sides that the Church must become mature, well constructed, and self-assured, and that each of its members must be filled by the fullness of Christ. It is not for nothing that Paul comes to speak again and again of this " being filled." Only the man who has been filled (we now speak of the individual) is the " perfect man," " well filled out," so to speak, in his soul, so that the currents and storms flow off him, because they can find no hold.

## LIVING THE TRUTH, TAKING ON THE FORM OF CHRIST (4:15)

... ¹⁵*so that we rather, doing the truth in love, grow into him in all regards, who is the head, Christ* ...

The operative word here means properly " being true," in the sense of "being truthful," "telling the truth." But one can "tell" the truth in something besides words; one can make it manifest, and proclaim it more impressively than with words, if one lives it and puts it into effect and so gives it visible embodiment (see Jn 3:21). That is probably what is meant here, because Paul adds "in love." Hence it is a call to tell the truth by deeds. To live up to the good tidings of Christ can be expressed in the one word "love" (Jn 17:22f.). But perhaps this idea of proclaiming the Gospel (by love in action) is taking us away from what Paul chiefly intends here. For he speaks of our *growing into Christ* (or up to Christ?). And this growth is to take place "in all regards." This may mean a growth which leaves no trait of conformity to Christ unconsidered, and at the same time a growth which everything can and should be made to serve. Here the "we" means the whole Church primarily, and the individual only in so far as he is a member of the whole, and fulfills in his growth his own particular and unique task. We might perhaps say: To the individual, the call is to grow into Christ, to the whole body, to grow up to the full Christ.

*Still It Is Christ Who Brings about the Growth of His Body (4:16)*

... *¹⁶from whom the whole body is knit together and held together through every joint of the support furnished, according to the power which is measured out to each part. Thus he effects the growth of the body, to the building-up of himself in love.*

In conclusion, Paul brings out once more, in its full force, the thought that *Christ,* the head, is the source of all growth in the

Church. It is he "*from whom the whole body is knit together and held together.*" This work, however, is not done directly, but by means of all sorts of joints, links, and ligaments. What the metaphor "joint" or "ligament" stands for is explained in the addition, "joint of services rendered," "support furnished" —one might almost say, "furnishing." The word meant originally the monetary support for the cost of the chorus in the Greek theatre. This *mutual support* between each member is the means whereby Christ binds his body together. It is really he, though the individual lends his support. But the individual does so in the power of, and " according to the measure of " the grace which Christ imparts to him for this task.

The clause, "*according to the power which is measured out to each part,*" clearly echoes 4:7, and takes up again the thought of that verse: " But to each of us grace was given according to the measure of the gift of Christ." Paul speaks in both places of the different " amounts " allotted to each individual, with which he makes his contribution to the whole work.

This reference to 4:7, which Paul clearly thought so important, has made the sentence too long, so that there is an involuntary change of subject. The original subject was the "whole body," but now it is Christ. Christ "*effects the growth of the body, to the building-up of himself in love.*" Love is mentioned once more in its isolated and yet so comprehensive place apart. But it becomes clear at once that it is fundamentally Christ's love which is at work in the mutual love of the members. And Paul insists once more that love is the decisive power at work in building up the body of Christ, by taking up again the thought of 4:15, " doing the truth in love, we will grow into him who is the head, Christ."

## Christian Life in Contrast to the Life of the Heathen (4:17-24)

The exhortatory part of the epistle began with the earnest entreaty to preserve the unity of the Spirit, and went on to reinforce this entreaty by enlarging upon the work of building up in this one body of Christ. The length of this passage—more than sixteen verses—shows that here we have one of the main interests of the Apostle. Now, before Paul passes on to particular admonitions. there comes a section which deals systematically with the situation and duties of the Christian. It contrasts his present Christian state with his heathen past.

### Heathen Life (4:17-19)

*[17]This then I say, imploringly, in the Lord, that you should no longer lead a life such as the heathens do in the worthlessness of their thinking, [18]darkened as they are in their intellect, estranged from the life of God on account of the ignorance that reigns in them, and on account of the hardness of their hearts; [19]for, dead to all moral feelings, they have given themselves over to vice, and practice all kinds of uncleanness in their lust to possess.*

The connecting particle " therefore " links the following once more to the moving considerations offered in the foregoing. Faced with such tasks in the Church and the world, in the Church for the world, bound so very personally to Christ and his work, —must not the Christian feel that this will make severe demands on his moral life, since his calling is so great? He is indeed called, but his call takes him out of a world and a way of life which has marked him for perhaps decades and which does not cease, even after his baptism, to put forward its claims, to offer its services, to beguile and cajole him. His past can still tempt and allure even the " new creature," all the more so since this past is still a living presence in all his surroundings. No wonder, then, that Paul urges his Christians, indeed " *conjures* " them solemnly " *in the Lord* "—who is the real speaker behind this exhortation—not to live any longer as the heathens do. Obviously, the warning was needed! Paul now goes on to sketch briefly and trenchantly the elements and manifestations of the heathen way of life.

" . . . in the worthlessness of their thinking." This is what he puts first. No matter how much emphasis is laid upon charity —the question of the truth remains decisive. The " mind " of which Paul speaks means here the faculty of thought. It was given to man to enable him to grasp the truth and the reality, so that the known reality should be a light for him on his way, authoritative, giving his life a direction. What, therefore, is " worthlessness," " futility," " nothingness " in thinking? It means that this power of comprehension grapples with the void, and that what it thinks to grasp is nothing but deceit and delusion. In this " world of thought " God is thus no longer beginning, middle, and end, but an idol, the self.

But let us see how Paul himself fills in these general outlines. In the Epistle to the Romans, we have the terrifying declaration: " They are holding down the truth in their wickedness." The evil will is therefore the root of the matter. They could have known better, they did know better, but they did not *wish* to know, and hence they are holding down the truth. " They are inexcusable, because they knew God, and still refused to pay him due honor or thank him. Instead, they gave themselves over to futile speculations, and their foolish heart was darkened" (Rom 1:18. 21).

Here we have Paul himself explaining, with all desirable clarity, what he sums up briefly in our present text. The first cause of evil is the bad will which suppresses the truth and prescribes to the intellect what it must think. This may be hard, because the intellect knows the creator, and knows that it exists thanks to this creator, and that obedience and service should be the consequence of such thanks. But that is precisely what man cannot bear, in his will to independence. So he must manage without God and without the truth, in the "worthlessness of his thinking."

But the worst is that this way of thinking becomes a habit. It becomes easier and easier to take illusion for reality. The light that once was there has been dimmed. Hence the description goes on in Ephesians: "*darkened as they are in their intellect*," parallel to which runs: "*estranged from the life of God on account of their ignorance*." The "life of God" here means human existence, as it was planned and willed by God: bestowed by God, filled by God, directed towards God. This is the truth. For this were we built. Only there are we "at home." Now, however, Paul says of the heathen that they are "estranged" or exiled from this spiritual homeland. This is worse and more terrifying than to say that they are just far from it or away from it. Even when far away, one can still be homesick, and this longing can prepare the way for the return home. But to be "estranged" from the life of God, to reject one's own home—that is horrifying. Paul adds: "on account of the ignorance that is in them." It has become now really ignorance, it is no longer "the *will* not to know" about the truth. Ignorance is indeed darkness, and the "hardened heart" is death.

"... *on account of the hardness of their hearts*." The "heart" is the whole man, thinking, feeling, striving. To be responsive to every call of the good, the beautiful, the divine, the homeward—that would be the " tender " heart, the way it should be. But the heart of the pagan in question is no longer on the wave length of what it was really made for, and so it has no standards at all. It has grown empty and poor, and thus hungry and thirsty, starving to fill itself, but now with things that can never satisfy its heart.

" . . . for, dead to all moral feelings, they have given themselves over to vice, and practice all kinds of uncleanness in their lust to possess." This evokes once more the passage that we have already quoted from the Epistle to the Romans. There, to be sure, it is God who has delivered the heathens over to " uncleanness," the crimes of their hearts (1:24). But above and beyond " impurity " in the strict sense there is a whole catalogue of other vices which follows there (1:29ff.). The whole passage only sets out more copiously what our present text names so tersely as " all sorts of uncleanness in their lust to possess." The somewhat bold translation we have given, " lust to possess," is an endeavor to render the Greek word " *pleonexia*," which means, strictly speaking, avarice, but here must obviously include much more. In our usage, the word " avarice " is understood only of greed for money and goods. Here, however, as the context demands, it must be the equivalent of an avid desire for all sorts of possessions, from which man hopes to fill up his emptiness—which he can never succeed in doing along such paths.

## *Christian Life (4:20-24)*

[20]*But you—that is not how you have learned Christ,* [21]*in as*

*much as you have heard of him and been instructed in him, as the truth is in Jesus, *²²*to lay aside, in the sense of past behavior, the old man who is perishing in deceptive lusts, *²³*to renew yourselves in mind and spirit, *²⁴*and to put on the new man who has been created according to God, in true righteousness and holiness.*

## LEARNING CHRIST (4:20–21)

"*But you—that is not how you have learned Christ.*" It is a pity to see the stylistic harshness of this expression smoothed away, and translated as something like "were you not told of Christ?" In the original text, in fact, the expression sounds just as surprising. And how can the hearing of the message, the receiving of catechetical instruction, be better expressed, in its depth and essence, than by the words "learn Christ"? This supposes, of course, that Christ is preached and nothing else, that Christ is the all-predominant figure in catechetical instruction, that all teaching points to him, and that he alone bestows the consecration and the personal warmth on all the rest. This is the only concept of preaching and catechism which could lead to the formulation of "learning Christ."

And there is something else at the bottom of this surprising way of putting things. For Paul, "learning Christ" means learning *a way of life*. Now that means, if we keep strictly to the mind of the Apostle, not so much—and certainly not only—what we call the "imitation of Christ," which makes us think chiefly of the figure of Christ in the Gospels as a model to be copied. No, "learning Christ," in a way which gives rise to a way of life, for Paul means primarily to have a grasp of Christ's work. It is to know what God has done through him with us, God's plan of salvation—somewhat as Paul was able to delineate it for us at the beginning of this epistle—as it goes forth from eternity and prepares us "in him" and "through him" for an eternity. That was the note sounded by the theme of Christ, when it occurred fifteen times in the eleven verses of the opening hymn. That is what Paul means when he speaks of "learning Christ."

We remember, no doubt, the prayer which he offered in behalf of his faithful (1:17ff.). It was for a "spirit of wisdom and revelation," for "enlightened eyes of the heart, so that they might know . . ." And then he spoke of the greatness of our hope, of the incomprehensible power of the resurrection of Christ, destined to be exerted on us believers; of the glory and primacy of Christ; and then of Christ the head, who fills his body, the Church, with all his own fullness of divine life. All *that* is meant by "learning Christ." And that this gives certain consequences for the conduct of life is made clear at once by the very structure of the whole epistle. First comes the doctrine, and then the exhortation. Thus the expression "learning Christ" renders with masterly brevity the fact that the Pauline message is totally centered on Christ.

"*To hear*" *Christ*. Grammatically, the phrase impels us to understand "to hear of Christ, about Christ." But are not perhaps two concepts interwoven here: Christ as the object of whom one speaks, and Christ as the person who in the last resort himself speaks to the soul with and in the preaching? Protestants have developed on this point a whole "theology of the word," and they miss it among us Catholics. For them, the word of God has practically the nature of a sacrament. Just as in baptism it is Christ who baptizes, just as in the Eucharist he makes himself present, so too it is he who, as the word is preached, addresses men " in, through, and under " the words of the preacher. Without trying to make a " theology " of it, we can say that the concept is profound and estimable, and well fitted to fill us with reverence, confidence, and a sense of responsibility, whenever we are present at the preaching of the word, either as hearers or as speakers.

". . . *instructed in him*." We can say in English that we have been instructed in such and such a subject, say, in the faith, but not that we have been instructed " in a person." Thus we would have here the same startling construction as in the words " learning Christ." To be instructed in him would then mean to be at home in everything that Christ is, and in everything that has to do with Christ; it would mean to have mustered the whole subject of the God-man, and to have learned how to live by him.

But that is a matter of English usage. In the Greek original, the words " [to be instructed] in him " can hardly be understood except in the Pauline sense of " in Christ," and hence, by the mandate, the authority of Christ, and indeed, to have received instruction which springs from union with him. If so, the words " in as much as you have been instructed in him " would be the equivalent of: if your teacher was speaking " in Christ " and if you received the word as men who are " in Christ." Both are necessary if a truth of the faith is to be accepted in such a way that it becomes effective. This spiritual kinship is needed between him who speaks and him who hears. A supernatural organ of sense is needed in order to be able to hear " spiritually " (see 1 Cor 2:13f.).

" But in the process of Christian instruction, as so described, is everything to depend upon the subjective attitude of him who is speaking and him who is listening? We can and we must go further. The objective reliability of "being instructed in him" is only guaranteed if we may make "in Christ" the equivalent of "in the Church."

"... *as the truth is in Jesus.*" The strong emphasis laid upon "him," "in him," was already enough to give the impression that the readers of the epistle could have been told about another Christ. This impression is now confirmed by the additional phrase, "as the truth is in Jesus." Very exceptionally, Paul here lays the emphasis upon "Jesus," where as elsewhere in Ephesians he always speaks of "Christ." In fact, the wording of the thought seems to be determined here by a glance at (Gnostic) opponents, for whom "Christ" is not simply indentical with Jesus of Nazareth.

In the First Epistle of John, we have clear traces of such early Gnostic currents of thought. It is true that we know very little about this early form of Gnosis, but from later Gnosticism we can deduce certain basic principles. 1) The more marked the hostility to everything material, the less is one inclined to have anything to do with God's becoming man. 2) The more redemption is transferred to the region of knowledge (*gnosis*), the less significance has the redemptive work of Christ in his death and resurrection. 3) The more this salvific *gnosis* is expected as a personal illumination from God, the less sympathy and understanding is brought to bear for the revelation which came only once, in the Son of God become man historically. —When such streams of thought dominate, it is understandable that Jesus of Nazareth, the redeemer whose expiatory death and resurrection was a unique historical event, could become " a more or less mythological image."

John was aware of this danger, and he fought is vigorously. "Who is the liar, except him who denies that Jesus is the

Christ?" (I Jn 2:22). Or: " Every spirit who acknowledges that Jesus Christ has come in the flesh, is from God . . ." (4:2). We see here clearly that the early Christians knew of schools of thought to which the thought of an incarnation of the redeemer (" Christ ") in the historical Jesus of Nazareth remained distasteful and painful.


## PUTTING OFF THE OLD MAN (4:22)

" . . . *to lay aside, in the sense of past behavior, the old man."* Such a radically new life is demanded of Christians that Paul can speak of " laying aside " not this or that fault, but the old man as a whole, and of " putting on the new man."

But according to Paul himself, did not both take place at baptism? " All of you, because you have been baptized into Christ, *have* put on Christ " (Gal 3:27). We have here a phenomenon which is well known in the writings of Paul. He frequently states that something has already happened, and then again, that it is still to come. The two thoughts are perhaps found closest together in the Epistle to the Colossians: " *Lay aside* anger, bitterness . . . , since you *have put off* the old man . . . and *have put on* the new, who is constantly being renewed . . . according to the image of his creator." And immediately after, we read: " Therefore *put on* . . . heartfelt compassion. . . ," that is, the moral attitude which corresponds to the existence of grace (Col 3:8-12). So, too, in our present text. The divine life which God by his grace has " impressed " upon us—the image of his Son—is now to be " expressed " in the Christian life as the Christian is shaped " to the likeness of the Son of God " (Rom 8:29). Being strives for action, force strives to exert itself, and life wills to be lived. If we allow this being, this force, this life to manifest themselves as their nature demands, then indeed we shall really " put on " in effect this " new man " whom we have already put on in our being.

It should not be too difficult, Paul thinks, to lay aside the old man, since he leads to death and destruction. He is " the old man, who is destroying himself in deceptive lusts." They are deceptive lusts, because they seem to promise, indeed do promise, fullness of life, and give the illusion of it: and in the end bring only death.

## Putting on the New Man (4:23–24)

" . . . ²³*to renew yourselves in mind and spirit,* ²⁴*and to put on the new man.*"

As a sort of prelude to putting on the new man, Paul now calls for a " self-renewal " in mind and spirit, literally, " in the spirit of your minds " (=intellect). Much remains obscure here. Is the Holy Spirit meant? But then why is he called the spirit of the faculty of thought? Perhaps we should understand this genitive (" of your minds ") as explicative? If so, the intellect, the faculty of thought itself would be intended, but in the sense in which it can also be called " *pneuma* " (spirit) in the language of Paul. And then it would mean our thinking, in so far as it is directed by the influence of the Holy Spirit, " Christian " thinking, thought guided by faith. This is what is to be constantly renewed, as it keeps itself always open and submissive to the ever new influences of the Spirit.

What we really have here is the parallel picture, but in reverse, to Paul's description of the heathen way of life, where "worthlessness of thought" came in the first place. It was this which was basic in making the life of a heathen a heathen life. If Christian life is to take its place, this very way of thinking must change, a real "change of mind" must take place. Thought that grasps reality must take the place of "thought that clutches at nothingness." But since this reality is the reality presented by faith, the renewal can only be effected in the Spirit.

It is consoling to see that Paul, too, is well aware that in the Christian life all is not achieved with one single spring, one single conversion, but that we are constantly faced with decisions, constantly turning to God—and above all, that our thinking in the faith (the source of our action) needs continual renewal. Here are the biblical grounds for the need of meditation, of becoming familiar with the word of God, of living consciously in a "spiritual" atmosphere. We keep on course by perpetual vigilance. We do not hold to our course automatically. And the stronger the winds, the fiercer the currents which run counter to the course we have charted, the more need we have of such pilotry (see 4:14).

Only when this foundation, our understanding of the faith, has been secured, can we really begin *to put on the new man*. This, too, will always call for constantly renewed efforts. It is surprising, therefore, that we do not read here the tense of duration and repetition, as in the verb "renewing" oneself, but the tense which indicates something that happens once for all. This may be connected with the imagery behind "putting on," which is a transient activity, the object of which is the man who has been put on; the final result is before the mind.

In the language of Paul, the "new man" is the man "in Christ," "newly created in Christ for good works" (2:10), "the inward man " (3:16), whose strength is the Spirit of God, the man who has Christ dwelling in him by faith (3:17). In our present text, he is said to have been "*created according to God*," that is, in the words of the Epistle to the Colossians, " according to the image of his creator " (Col 3:10). We may, however, perhaps take the verb " create " in its literal sense of " founding," " laying foundations." Then we are ordained to the likeness of God in Christ, and we have to put it into effect " in true righteousness and holiness," that is, in such righteousness and holiness as correspond to the truth, the God-given reality.

## The New Life in Love (4:25—5:2)

Up to now, Paul has first spoken of the unity and growth of the Church for the length of sixteen verses, and then for eight verses of the fundamental difference between the heathen and the Christian man. Only now does he come to individual admonitions. They are all more or less in the service of love, and directed against everything that is incompatible with love and peace in common life.

### *What Love Does Not Do (4:25–31)*

Strictly speaking, this heading is not comprehensive enough, because Paul also adds in every case what love does.

#### LOVE DOES NOT LIE (4:25)

*²⁵Therefore lay aside the lie, and speak the truth, each one with his neighbor, for we are members of one another.*

Why, we may ask, does *truthfulness* come at the top? One might well imagine that it was occasioned by the final word of the preceding verse: "in righteousness and holiness of truth." But the reason goes deeper, as the parallel admonition in the Epistle to the Colossians shows (3:8f.). There the warning "do not lie to one another" has a very special place. It is not placed simply in the same line as anger, bitterness, and so on. The warning against falsehood begins a completely new phrase, and is attached only to the discarding of the old man and the assumption of the new: "Do not lie to one another! For you have put off the old man . . ." Falsehood in business and behavior may indeed have been a major element in the southeastern surroundings of the early Church. But swindling, deviousness, double-dealing, and falsehood will always be the hallmark of the age and society where the sense of the inner bonds between men has been lost, and they are no longer conscious of being dependent upon one another and existing for one another. But it was this social sense that Christianity brought to an individualistic world, offering it a new motive of undreamt-of depth: you are not only equals, you are not only brothers, you are members of one body, and that is the sacred body of Christ, who binds you all together and makes you "one person" in himself. But the lie divides, sends up partitions, and is therefore an offense not only against one's brother, but against the whole body and Christ its head.

## LOVE IS NOT ANGERED (4:26–27)

*[26]If you are angry, still, do not commit sin! Do not let the sun go down on your anger. [27]And do not leave any room for the devil.*

It is dangerous to keep up ill-feeling. It eats its way in, it casts around—everything can be made to serve it as new nourishment. It gives room to the devil. It invites him, as it were, to make of us men blinded, or at least unbalanced, by hostility, and apply us to his own ends, which are always disturbance and destruction. These words " leave the devil no room " have a counterpart, and a remedy, if one wills, in those other words of the Epistle to the Romans: " Leave room for *the* anger," that is, for the judgment of God, and give up trying to enforce your rights by yourselves. " Vengeance is mine, I will repay, says the Lord " (Rom 12:19). Justice is only the business of the God who knows all. Be merciful, if you want to be just.

## LOVE DOES NOT STEAL (4:28)

*28Let the thief give up stealing, and instead, earn money by hard manual labor, so that he may have something to share with the needy.*

We are perhaps surprised to find that it is taken so much for granted that thieves are admitted to the community, thieves who had been used to living without working, and who were not ready to give up their habits completely when they became Christians. This may be surprising, but the confidence of Paul is still more surprising. He takes it for granted that he can put a lofty goal before the former thief. Not only is he not to be a burden to anybody (I Thes 4:12), and not only is he to gain his livelihood by his own work (that is not even mentioned); he is to earn money (literally, " the good "), presumably possessions, perhaps even good money. And he is to do this not in order to be well and comfortably off, but to give some of it away to those who are in need. What optimism! How many of us are there, who have never been thieves, who work with such an end in view?

## Love does not sin by evil talk (4:29)

*²⁹Let no foul talk pass your lips, but rather a good word to edify, where there is need, so that it may be of benefit to its hearers.*

The *good word* is therefore the one that builds up, that in one way or another, be it ever so quietly, will be one of those " services rendered " of which it was said in 4:16, that Christ used them to establish and build his body. When Paul then speaks of the " good," edifying word as a " benefit," using for " benefit " the expression ordinarily kept for " grace," we are justified in finding two thoughts suggested by the term. One is the thought of a benefit conferred by one member upon another, the other that this benefit ultimately derives from the love of Christ. The good word in the right place, even dealing with purely human affairs, still extends effectively, from the Christian standpoint, into the region of great, holy, and divine things.

## Love does not grieve the Holy Spirit (4:30)

*³⁰And do not grieve the Holy Spirit of God, by whom you were sealed for the day of redemption.*

This sentence gives the impression of being an exclamation which belongs as a sort of link both to what precedes and follows. The thought comes as a surprise. Paul does not remind his readers once more of their great hope (1:14), though this theme is vigorously at work throughout the epistle. Nor does he use the thought as a warning "to preserve the unity of the Spirit in love" (4:3). Instead, this *Spirit of God,* the "seal" of our hope, is presented and experienced here so personally for the first time, that Paul at once asks his readers to try not to grieve him, not to "pain" him, as we would say. This is something new, all the more so as this Spirit has been spoken of hitherto so much as if it were an instrument. No matter how incorrect it may be, from the strictly theological point of view, to say that the Spirit of God experiences joy or pain at what we do—Paul has no such misgivings! He thinks and speaks in human terms, using the only language which is on our own level and understandable to us, especially to the simple Christian. To "gladden" and "not to hurt" some person who is close to us, to whom we owe an immense amount—that is still one of the noblest motives that can direct all our conduct.

## LOVE DOES NOT ALLOW OF ANY MALICE (4:31)

*³¹Any trace of bitterness and resentment, of anger and disturbance and cursing—banish it from your midst, along with all malice.*

These, then, are the things by which one grieves the Holy Spirit, for they spoil our joys and disturb our peace. They are all part of the old man, who is not yet quite dead; they are part of the man who is closed in on himself and constricted within his own ego. Paul enumerates the mental attitudes—bitterness, resentment, anger—and what is said out loud: shouting and cursing. There is a source for all this, and it is to be found in malice. Hence the admonition: "Banish it all from your midst, along with all malice."

## What Love Does (4:32—5:2)

When Paul was speaking of what was contrary to love, he attached to each warning its positive counterpart. Now he speaks of love alone, and explains its nature.

### LOVE IS MERCIFUL AND CONCILIATORY (4:32)

*32But be kind to one another and full of compassion, and forgive each other, as God in Christ forgave you.*

Once more, it is *patient love* which is in the foreground, not merely because in our present context it provides the opposite of all irascibility, but because of its own nature. This is in keeping with Paul's ordinary way of envisaging the effects of love. In 4:2f., humility, meekness, patience, and tolerance came also in the first place. And in the "Song of Songs" to charity in I Cor 13:4-7, of the fifteen of the attributes of love there enumerated, no fewer than eight recount expressly what love does *not* do (" it is not jealous, is not puffed up "), and six further attributes deal with the patience of love (" bears all things, suffers all things "). Be therefore attached to one another in tolerant kindness.

Above all, *forgiveness*! This can be immensely hard for human beings, this forgiving, forgetting, passing over in silence. As a motive, Paul brings forward the forgiveness which every Christian has experienced on the part of God, a forgiveness that entails for him nothing less than resurrection from the dead (2:5). It is a forgiveness to which he owes his great hope as well as the true life. Finally, it is a forgiveness which, humanly speaking, cost God not a little, because his grace came to us " given in the well-beloved, in whom we have redemption through his blood, the remission of our sins " (1:6f.). Hence Paul says in the present text: " as God in Christ forgave you." The thought should never really be far from our minds, because we experience God's forgiveness day after day, and know how much we need it. After all, we pray for it, as Jesus himself taught us, in the Lord's Prayer. And we remember how insistently in the Gospel the Lord proclaimed the obligation of forgiving, and how urgent were the reasons he gave for it.

## By pardoning, it imitates the love of God and Christ (5:1-2)

*¹Be then imitators of God as beloved children, ²and walk in love, as Christ also loved you and delivered himself up for us as an offering and a sacrifice, as a fragrance sweet to God.*

By our act of forgiveness, we are enabled to imitate him who has first forgiven us, God. And we should do that " *as beloved children.*" For it is by watching his father, in order to copy him closely, that a child really shows himself the true child of his father. We think spontaneously of the climax of the Sermon on the Mount: "Be perfect, as your heavenly Father is perfect" (Mt 5:48), which is given in a form closer to our context by Luke: "Be therefore merciful, as your Father is merciful" (6:36). But the thought of our present text is enunciated most clearly in the commandment: Love your enemies, "that you may show yourselves to be children of your Father who is in heaven" (Mt 5:44).

A life so lived with one's eyes fixed on the Father is also *the* way of imitating Christ. It is an attitude which, in a mysteriously deeper sense, of course, was proper to the Son in a unique way. "The Son can do nothing of himself, but only whatever he sees the Father doing. Whatever he does, the Son does also in like manner" (Jn 5:19). Thus the man Jesus lived in the most profound "imitation of God," though in sacred Scripture "imitation" is hardly mentioned. But it speaks instead all the more insistently of "obedience" and of the fulfillment of the Father's will.

From the imitation of the merciful God, the horizon is now enlarged to take in the whole extent of Christian life, which is once more characterized by the word "love," and based upon the model of the loving sacrifice of Christ. That this "walk in love" really embraces the whole extent of Christian life becomes clear at once when we try to remind ourselves how often this formula occurs, even in the Epistle to the Ephesians. In this epistle, Paul has not only spoken of "forbearance in love" (4:2), but he has said that the Gospel, *the* truth, is lived up to only "in love" (4:15). Indeed, basically it is Christ himself who builds up his body "in love" (4:16)—in our love, in so far as it is active in and through the mutual love of the faithful. It is always

" fraternal charity "! Hence at the beginning of the epistle we took the first occurrence of the phrase in the same way, and saw that the immediate object of our election is the call " to be holy and blameless before him *in love* " (1:4).

The model of this love is the love of the Crucified. This points insistently to the fact that love means *sacrifice*, service, self-dedication which involves total self-sacrifice. For the sacrificial love of Christ is at once the model and the standard of our love: " Love one another, as I have loved you " (Jn 15:12). Whence comes the conclusion, so striking in its simplicity, and yet so telling, which the beloved disciple drew: " . . . he has laid down his life for us; and we likewise ought to lay down our lives for the brothers " (I Jn 3:16).

Paul had a reason for expressing the thought of Jesus' death on the cross in terms taken from the Old Testament terminology of sacrifice: " offering," " sacrifice," " a fragrance pleasing to God." Hence the train of thought in the last two verses would be as follows: the imitation of God takes the form, in the nature of things, of the imitation of Christ, and this in turn, in the mind of Paul, does not consist of this or that virtue, but ultimately and universally in copying Christ's sacrifice of his life. It is therefore the imitation of what is renewed day by day at the hands of the priest which should be verified in the life of all who offer and are offered in this common sacrifice.

# The New Life in Purity and Light (5:3–14)

Paul takes up a new topic. This time the main vice of paganism, fornication, is spoken of first, and it remains the dominant theme of the next five verses.

## The Works of Darkness and Their Consequences (5:3-8)

### THE MAIN VICES (5:3-4)

*³Fornication, however, and impurity of any kind, or avarice, must not be even mentioned among you, as is fitting for saints; ⁴filthiness, too, and foolish chatter and double-meaning jokes, all of which are unbecoming; but thanksgiving instead.*

By the words "Fornication . . . and impurity of any kind" a whole region is excluded from the Christian life. It is a region where men are all to prone to indulge human weakness, extending from the external sin of sexual satisfaction outside marriage to obscene talk and even to inward desires, as the parallel text of the Epistle to the Colossians completes the thought: "fornication, impurity, passion, evil desire" (3:5). Once more we have avarice coming beside fornication, where it has characteristically its fixed, almost conventional place in Paul. The text just quoted from the Epistle to the Colossians also continues with "and avarice, which is idolatry." The condemnation of *avarice* as idolatry is missing in our present text, but it is made up for shortly afterwards (5:5), where we find the "avaricious" beside the "licentious and impure," and where he is said to be "an idolater." On account of this constant association of fornication and avarice in the thought of Paul, commentators have been tempted to look for a vice under the Greek word which would have to do with sexual life, especially as the two concepts are combined, as it were, into one, as we saw in 4:19, where Paul spoke of "all sorts of impure acts, in avarice." However, we shall perhaps only do justice to the style of the Apostle if we keep each of the two vices as they are, namely, fornication and avarice, for we must bear in mind that for Paul the decisive element in both is clearly the lust, whether it be the lust for enjoyment or the lust for possessions. It condemns men to slavery anyway. The object of their desire becomes their god (Phil 3:19). All the same, only avarice is called idolatry, and not fornication. This is probably connected with the fact that the avaricious man is more master of himself, and that more conscious deliberation, indeed calculation, lies behind his actions.

Then we read that these three things, fornication, impurity, and avarice, "*must not be even mentioned among you.*" The words " not even " show clearly that Paul is aware that his expression is exaggerated. We could therefore render it, with the same exaggeration: " . . . they should not even be known to you by name." The sense would be: " they should never occur at all among you."

The reason for this is given very simply: "*as is fitting for saints.*" This supposes, of course, that Christians have a high concept of their state. They must have a keen sense of the fact that they are baptized into Christ and sealed by the Holy Spirit as his property. Hence they will know that they belong so closely to God, and are so much part of the region of the sacred, that to import anything profane and ungodly into this realm would be a sort of desecration, a robbery of sacred vessels and a sacrilege in a shrine. This is precisely what is explained in forcible terms in the First Epistle to the Corinthians, apropos of the sins of the flesh and the profanation of the human body.

Paul adds to this another group of three vices, which corresponds almost exactly to the first in the structure of the phrase. He has just spoken of " Fornication . . . impurity of any kind, or avarice." Now he says: " filthiness, too, and foolish chatter and double-meaning jokes." It is not quite clear what is meant by filthiness, foolish chatter, and double-meaning jokes, of which he goes on to speak at once. We may take it that this second triad belongs to the same category as the first, because only the latter is taken up again immediately afterwards (5:5), with the words " the fornicator, the impure, the avaricious."

Paul had already spoken of *indecent speech* in 4:29: " Let no foul talk pass your lips." However, there everything was treated of from the point of view of consideration for one's fellow men, and hence the contrast to " foul talk " was " a good word . . . of benefit to its hearers." In our present text, on the other hand, the moral conduct of the individual remains in the foreground.

Paul seems to feel deeply all misuse of divine gifts, of precious human faculties. This is true in general of licentiousness and avarice, but becomes particularly clear here, where it is not a matter of such basic essentials, but of misuse of human speech, which makes it possible for us to praise God publicly, and fulfill thereby its noblest task. But who would have thought of praise and thanksgiving as the opposite of foul talk?

The idea occurs unexpectedly here, but that only makes it all the more characteristic of Paul. Praise and thanksgiving are for him the basic attitude of the Christian. We could perhaps compare the text in the Epistle to the Colossians where he comes so surprisingly to speak of this gratitude. It says that Christians should be " firmly rooted in Christ, built up in him, growing strong in the faith . . . , *overflowing with thanksgiving* " (2:7). If we take Col 3:15 along with this, where " and be thankful! " crops up so suddenly, and many other texts of the same sort, then we can really affirm that gratitude to God is a basic interest of the Apostle, which dominates him so much that it forces itself upon him, in season or out of season, on every occasion.

## THE CONSEQUENCES OF THESE VICES (5:5-7)

*⁵For this you should know: no one that is a fornicator, or impure, or avaricious, which is the same as being an idolater, has any inheritance in the kingdom of Christ and God. ⁶Let no one deceive you with empty words, for the anger of God comes upon the children of disobedience because of these things. ⁷Have nothing to do with them.*

Here we find for once something that is not at all too common in Paul. He gives as a moral motive the thought of the *consequences of immoral life.* They cannot be taken seriously enough, for they are exclusion from the kingdom and heritage of God.

Paul had already spoken of the " Kingdom of God " in the Epistle to the Colossians. There we read that " God has rescued us from the power of darkness, and transferred us into the Kingdom of the Son of his love " (1:13). Here we see that the " Kingdom of God " is presented as the realm ruled by " his well-beloved Son " (see 1:6). But it is God who " redeems " us and transfers us into this kingdom of his Son, just as it is God who " has subjected all things to himself " (Eph 1:22). It is in this sense that " Kingdom of Christ and of God " is to be understood. In the realm where Christ rules, the realm that is subject to him, we have a share in the Kingdom of God, even at the present time, as it has already begun, essentially, though as yet secretly (Col 3:3). But what is now hidden will come to light in glory, for it is nothing but the life of Christ in us. Paul now says that the sinner is excluded from the Kingdom in both senses. They *will* not inherit the Kingdom of God, because they *have* at present no share in that heritage. This is the

Apostle's way of describing the objective conditions which are termed in theological language, much less forcibly, as the " state " or, as the case may be, the " loss of sanctifying grace."

"*Let no one deceive you with empty words, for the anger of God comes upon the children of disobedience because of these things.*" So there are other voices raised, to say that fornication and avarice do not matter. In themselves they do not matter, because they are simply the way man's nature lives out its bent; and they have no consequences that matter! "Let us eat and drink, for tomorrow we die " (I Cor 15:32). Paul admits that these voices from the world are right—" *if* the dead do not arise."

The "*empty words*" are those which have no reality behind them, but only the sort of thinking which snatches at the void. It is the way of thinking which is encouraged in every possible way by " the prince in the realm of the air, the spirit that is at work in the children of disobedience," the spirit which interprets the world as an independent being, which can and must be its own end and object, just like the men who live in it. "Do not let yourselves be misled!" cries the Apostle, for they are the voices of the Sirens, all the more dangerous because there is something in man which is only too ready to yield to them.

". . . these things," which the world takes so lightly are the very things " on account of which the anger of God comes upon *the children of disobedience.*" Anyone who adapts his life to their pattern has thereby left the kingdom of light into which he was brought when rescued, and has fallen once more into the power of darkness, and thus is subject to the judgment that will come upon it. "Have nothing to do with them!" because the danger you expose yourself to is too great.

The *anger of God* spoken of here is not only something in the future; no, it is already in action. Paul describes it in the Epistle to the Romans with a triple "therefore God has given them over," namely for themselves, to their lusts, in the most terrible and shameful slavery (see Rom 1:21-32).

The Apostle is clearly concerned here with over-liberal attitudes in moral matters, above all in sexual ethics. This is called libertinism, that is, a morality that can pass at will over every frontier. The same moral, or rather immoral, attitude can spring from very different and indeed seemingly contradictory presuppositions. A Gnostic exaggeration of the role of the spiritual could lead to matter and the flesh being left to their own devices: they are to go their own way, the only thing that matters is the spirit.

A false and one-sided way of understanding Paul's attitude to the Law and "good works" comes to the same result. Justification by faith alone could also be misinterpreted as meaning that faith is all the greater the fewer the works there are. This is the so-called "antinomianism," that is, anti-legalism, or rather, hostility to law. Luther found out by experience what his one-sided emphasis upon Pauline doctrine gave rise to in the moral life of the Christian people, and it was a sad experience for him. How do we feel about it when the Church tirelessly proclaims to the deaf ears of a whole world: fornication, impurity, avarice, "these are the things which will bring down the wrath of God on the children of disobedience"? Do we not also feel the terrifying tug of the temptation to find fault with Catholic morals (sexual and matrimonial ethics), and to declare its conceptions old-fashioned? One may think that shifts of accent are advisable, but *what* this moral doctrine teaches must remain inviolable. The anger of God is coming, and "these are the things which bring it down. Do not get yourselves mixed up with them!"

## Live as Children of Light (5:8-20)

### BEAR THE FRUITS OF THE LIGHT (5:8-10)

*⁸You were once darkness, but now [you are] light in the Lord. Walk therefore as children of the light; ⁹for the fruit of the light [consists of] all kinds of goodness and justice and truth. ¹⁰Decide upon that which is pleasing to the Lord . . .*

Paul rarely threatens his readers with the wrath of God, as in the preceding passage. He is much more interested in showing how the moral life of the Christian follows from the nature of Christian being. So, too, here once again. The words " you were " in the Greek have a special position of emphasis at the beginning of the phrase, and that is enough to imply that Christians are no longer what they were. Not only has a whole world been changed, but more, these very persons who *have been* darkness have now themselves *become light*. A new creation has taken place, the " man in Christ " has come into existence, one with him who is " the light of the world " (Jn 1:5; 8:12), and who can therefore say to his own: " You are the light of the world " (Mt 5:14).

" Walk therefore as children of the light . . ." *Children of the light* was the name given to Christians as early as the first epistle written by Paul: " You are all children of the light and children of the day " (I Thes 5:5). This use of " child " or " son " is a Semitic way of expressing a very intimate relationship, and it may be useful to recall its origin: Like father, like son. Habits of thought and ways of life are transmitted along with life and existence. " The child is father of the man." So also here: To stem from the light, to be oneself the light—this is the obligation.

Light must shine, and this shining is nothing else than everything that can be called "*goodness*" and "*justice*" and "*truth*."

These are the three most general terms possible for *moral perfection*. Any one of them by itself would have been enough to indicate the whole scale, even if Paul had not put in " all kinds of." " Truth " means a life in accord with reality. If this inner reality of the Christian, this nature that strives to be effective in action, is understood and accomplished as the will of God, as law, then what once was called " truth " is now called " justice." Finally, the term for " goodness " again means righteousness, but perhaps with an overtone of love and kindness. So the three of them are really not " fruits," but, as it says in our text, " the fruit " of the light.

"*Decide upon that which is pleasing to the Lord.*" Paul has spoken of "the fruit" of the light. But this "fruit" is of a special nature. It does not grow automatically out of the goodness of the tree that bears it. Its bearer must busy himself constantly with examining, choosing, and *deciding* upon " what is pleasing to the Lord." He must not try to please himself or to please others. The only rule and standard in such a choice is to try to please the Lord.

## Lead to the Light Those Who Are in Darkness (5:11-14)

... *[11]and take no part in the barren works of darkness, or better still, expose them; [12]for what is done by them in secret one would blush to mention. [13]But everything that is exposed begins to shine under the light; for everything that is illumined is light. [14]Hence it is said " Awake, you who are sleeping, rise up from the dead, and Christ will illumine you."*

... "*the barren works of darkness.*" Paul does not now speak —as he did about the fruits of the light—of the "fruits" of darkness. It seems as though the metaphor would do them too much honor. He only speaks of "works" of darkness, and adds at once that they are "barren works." From the human point of view, they may be achievements or even mighty feats, but if they stem from darkness they can only spread darkness, and every apparent gain is dupery and delusion. The fact that the works are here called "barren" shows that, when speaking earlier on of the "fruit" of the light, Paul was not thinking only of their having been produced by the light, but also of their being of benefit to others, since they are "fruits." Coming from the light, they also spread light.

"*... or better still, expose them.*" The word translated as "expose" is used in very different senses in the New Testament ("convince," "rebuke"). H. Schlier compares our text—very happily, it seems—with I Cor 14:24, and finds the process in question analyzed there into three steps: one tests, one brings to light, one "transfers"—the word here being taken in its original sense of "bring over," which would mean in our present case "convert."

"*... everything that is exposed begins to shine under the light; for everything that is illumined is light.*" Since this translation is not really clear, and the original Greek is still less clear, the only thing to do is to ponder what is meant, starting from what is certain. We have the duty of "exposing" (or "converting": 5:11b), and then at the end the reason for it, the desired goal: "for [the object exposed or converted] is light." If this train of thought is to provide a worthy insight, then this "being illumined," this "coming to light" cannot simply mean that the persuasive words of the Christian simply drags the hidden scandal into the light of day, and thus shows it up in all its shamefulness. Who would be prepared to say that shame laid bare has become light by the very fact of being laid bare? Paul must be speaking, no matter how compressed his train of thought, of a showing up where *the* light, Christ, is triumphantly active, and brings about conversion. In fact, Christ does appear immediately afterwards as the light (5:14b).

It remains obscure, however, how Paul could then state as a general principle, *in this sense*, that " everything that is exposed begins to shine under the light." And yet this sense is demanded by the additional explanation: " for everything that is illumined is light." However, that Paul is really thinking of the conversion of sinners is made perfectly clear by the self-explanatory quotation now added: " Hence it is said: ' Awake, you who are sleeping, rise up from the dead, and Christ will illumine you '." It is thought that this passage, which sounds like part of a hymn, may come from a baptismal liturgy, and be part of an acclamation addressed to those about to be baptized. For they were on the point of entering upon a new life, as different from their earlier existence as clear-sighted wakefulness is from heavy sleep, as the life of the resurrection is from death. And their new life will be lived in new world, under a new sun: Christ.

## Seek in Wisdom the Will of God (5:15-17)

<sup>15</sup>*Pay careful heed, therefore, to the way you behave, not as fools, but as wise men,* <sup>16</sup>*exploiting the time to the full, for the days are evil.* <sup>17</sup>*Do not therefore be stupid, but try to understand what the will of the Lord is.*

The conjunction " therefore " may refer to the illumination

experienced in baptism, which has just been recalled. A new life has been given in new light, though of course it is to be led with full consciousness and responsibility. Christians had already been charged with the task of examining each step, and deciding in each case upon "what is pleasing to the Lord." Here, too, the first thing thought of is a correct grasp of what may be the will of God in each case. Hence the exhortation, which almost sounds like a warning, to "pay heed," to "see to it" with all possible diligence. Things are not so simple. There are inward (2:3) and outside (2:2) forces at work trying to dim the light, obscure the view, and block or complicate the correct decision. They should not live as "fools," since they are no longer simpletons, once the riches of God's grace has streamed over and into them, giving them the essence of all wisdom and insight through the revelation of the mystery of God's will (1:8f.). They are instead to conduct themselves as "wise men." The presence of the true wisdom should be patent in their lives, which will not be a careless, thoughtless affair of living for the day, but a deliberate effort to "exploit the time to the full." The Greek word "*kairos*" means more than one's "time." It means the contents of this time, the situation it creates, the opportunities it offers. We must make full use of these opportunities in view of our final end, we must make the best we can of every situation. That is what it means "exploiting the time to the full."

That is wisdom, and very necessary "... *for the days are evil.*" A thought dominant first in Jewish tradition and then in the Gospels makes itself felt here: that the Last Days, being the birth-pangs of a new world, bring "woes" with them, distress and tribulation of all kinds. It is the Evil One, summoning up the last resources of his defeated forces, who makes the days "evil." This "evil," which can cause such sharp distress, means that men are exposed to assault, temptation, and danger. We must be able to see the cross in all this evil, to find the way to life in all that is bent on destruction. It is for this that wisdom is necessary.

The Apostle's warning is vehement. Hence the repetition: "Do not therefore be stupid." The will of God alone! Knowledge of it is the opposite of foolishness. The will of God is decisive in everything that we have to do, to sacrifice, or to suffer. Where is the Christian to procure this knowledge of the will of God and the readiness to perform it? How is he to grow strong in such knowledge?

## Let yourselves be filled by the Holy Spirit (5:18-20)

[18]*And do not get drunk on wine, for therein lies destruction, but let yourselves be inebriated with the Spirit.* [19]*Speak to one another in psalms and hymns and chants inspired by the Spirit, sing to the Lord in your hearts and give him praise.* [20]*Give thanks to God and the Father at all times and for everything, in the name of our Lord Jesus Christ.*

The warning not to get drunk on wine comes as a real surprise. If this was meant as a continuation of the list of individual warnings begun earlier (4:25), we should expect a plea for moderation, as a counterpart to excessive drinking. But in fact the counterpart is given as being *inebriated with the Spirit,* and Paul goes on to deal with activities which can hardly be imagined as taking place outside the assemblies where the community gathers for worship.

But could a warning against excessive drinking have really

led to the thought of "high spirits" among the assembled community? Hardly, or if so, only if it is a matter of the drinking of wine which went with the common meals of the community. On this point, as a matter of fact, Paul had had to complain of disorders in Corinth: "Some go hungry, while others gorge themselves [literally: "are drunk"]" (I Cor 11:21). In this context, the mental association of bodily and spiritual inebriation would be conceivable, indeed obvious. Thus we have confirmation of the idea that Paul is actually thinking here of the liturgical life of the community. And, as we may gather from the context, he sees the liturgy as the place where each individual can draw upon the faith of the community, to renew himself constantly "in spirit and mind" (4:23), the place where he wins such insight into the will of God as will enable him to endure "the evil days" wisely, that is, as a real Christian.

Paul says of heavy drinking that there is *asotia* in it, which can mean a hopeless situation, *without refuge*, though also debauchery, dissipation. We are probably to think rather of the first of these meanings, which reminds us how people are tempted to "take refuge" in drink when some great trouble comes upon them. Yes, the Christian should really be relieved of the day's burden for a while, and be allowed to live "in another world." But it should be in the world where the Spirit can carry him off, in the most varied ways and degrees—as a distant foretaste of the life in God towards which we are going.

Where the community is gathered for worship, the Spirit fills the heart, but Christians must open their hearts to him ("let yourselves be filled by the Spirit"), and he will loosen their tongues in psalms and hymns and chants. This may be for all to sing together the well-known texts, but more probably, for impromptu alternating choruses, calling and responding to one another, in a holy emulation to praise God more and more. This singing is said to be " spiritual " in the full meaning of the word, namely, as coming from the Spirit, as filled by the Spirit and transmitting the Spirit.

But, Paul does not forget to add, that what gives these songs of praise their true value is neither the voice nor the delivery nor the perfection of their form. What counts is the inward " singing in the heart," which is prelude and accompaniment to the actual performance, —that inward song which is directed wholly to the Lord alone: " Sing to the Lord in your hearts and give him praise." And as if it were not already embodied in hymn and chant, Paul gives once more the note and the theme explicitly: " Give thanks to God and the Father at all times for everything [everybody?], in the name of our Lord Jesus Christ."

The word for " give thanks " here is " *eucharistein*." Are we to think of the great prayer of the Eucharist (the Preface of our Mass), and hence of the liturgical celebration of the Last Supper? This could be likely enough, in a passage which actually deals with the community as a congregation and divine worship. All the same, it would rather appear that the thought of the Apostle is already leading us back to the daily life of Christians, and to the *basic sentiment of Christian existence* which he has so much at heart: an attitude of jubilant thankfulness which praises God always and everywhere and for all things.

The words " at all times " seem to point to this interpretation, though the thought of the celebration of the Eucharist may be in the background, as the climax of this thanksgiving and the source whence this sentiment is to be renewed. We are reminded of I Thes 5:16-18: " Be joyful always, pray without ceasing, give thanks in every matter." Hence it is also doubtful whether we are to translate the text in our present verse as " for everybody " or "for everything." Both have a profound sense. To give thanks "for everybody" would be a very fitting expression of the Christian sense of belonging to one another: the joy of possessing salvation inspires us with gratitude for the presence of that salvation in our brothers. But the other interpretation, "thanksgiving for all things," would also be an expression of something that is profoundly Christian. It would voice the faith that sees the Father behind all things (our thanks go to "God and the Father"), and that knows that "to those who love God, *all things* work together unto good" (Rom 8:28).

## The Christian Household (5:21—6:9)

After speaking of the congregation at worship, Paul takes up the subject of the Christian family. The "family," as the word was understood in antiquity, was the whole household, husband and wife, children and slaves. They are all bound by one basic law, which Paul puts at the beginning as a sort of heading for the passage:

*²¹Be subject to one another in the fear of Christ.*

But here is something as surprising as it is significant: this heading forms gramatically the last member of the preceding passage, where the dominant idea was put in the imperative: "let yourselves be filled by the Spirit." This was expounded as: "speaking to one another . . . singing . . . giving thanks . . ." And now, as though continuing the same line of thought, we have "subject to one another," "submitting to one another." Thus the thought passes imperceptibly from divine worship to the *everyday life of the family*. Paul could hardly show more clearly how automatically he takes it for granted that Christian life is one indivisible entity, and that it may not consist of two different spheres: church and home, Sundays and weekdays, liturgy and life. They go together and must penetrate one another. Divine worship gives an ever deeper understanding of God's will, and the strength to carry it out. And on the other hand, life as it is lived, with its joys and sorrows, its successes and failures, its hopes and cares, is what the Christian brings with him when he appears before God in the liturgy along with his brethren.

We have a text in the Epistle to the Colossians which strikes the same note, so that the two texts confirm and explain one another. There the mention of the sentiment of gratitude leads us, as it were, into the assembly of the community, where this Christian attitude comes out in a special way: " Instruct one another and encourage one another, in all wisdom. Sing thankfully to God in your hearts, with psalms, hymns, and chants inspired by the Spirit." And here also, only more clearly, the whole range of everyday life is at once taken up: " And whatever you do, in word or work, do all in the name of Jesus, the Lord, thanking God the Father through him " (Col 3:16f.).

For Paul, the Christian household is built upon the just subordination of its members. That is, of course, true of every other well-ordered family also. The difference in a Christian family is that this submission, imposed or rather demanded by nature, is practiced " *in the fear of Christ*," that is, in holy reverence for Christ the Lord. That gives a new consecration to the whole of life. It makes submission, which men ordinarily find so hard, appear as something easy. It reconciles submission with the dignity of the human person. The right order of things is given a basis to support it, even where otherwise the incompetence of those in command would bring this structure into danger.

## Wife and Husband (5:22–33)

### WIVES, BE SUBJECT TO YOUR HUSBANDS, AS THE CHURCH TO CHRIST (5:22–24)

*[21Be subject to one another in the fear of Christ.] 22Wives, be subject to your husbands as to the Lord. 23For the husband is the head of the woman, just as Christ, too, is head of the Church, he, the saviour of the body. 24Indeed, just as the Church is subject to Christ, so should wives be to their husbands in everything.*

Wives must be subject to their husbands *as to the Lord*. In English " as " only indicates a comparison. If we wished to indicate the reason for the action, we should have to say " in as much as " [the husband stands for] the Lord. The Greek particle can mean either, and no doubt the notion of giving the reason is predominant here. It is an application of the phrase " in the fear of the Lord." The wife, by submitting to her husband, exercises an act of submission to Christ.

" *For the husband is the head of the woman, just as Christ, too, is the head of the Church, he, the saviour of the body.*" Marriage should be a copy of the relationship of Christ to his Church. Just as Christ is the head of his Church, so too, the husband must be for the wife. Under the word " head " we are most probably to think primarily of the position of lord and master. Christ, of course, as head of the Church, is far more than that. He is also the source of its life, the principle and the final end of its growth, which, needless to say, does not come into question for the husband as regards his wife.

Undoubtedly, Paul wishes to eliminate from the very start all trace of harshness from the authoritative position of the husband.

He wishes to exclude any idea of self-will, and self-seeking misuse. Hence he adds the rather surprising comment: " Christ, the saviour of his body." The higher position of the man must therefore be entirely directed to the " salvation " of the woman, just as it is with Christ in regard to the Church. This is how Paul sees the relationship on the side of the husband. The same thought is now taken up again from the point of view of the wife. " Yes, just as the Church is subject to Christ, so should wives be to their husbands in all things." No doubt, the very fact that the principle is twice formulated is meant to exclude all misunderstanding. The Apostle attributes the authoritative and leading role in marriage to the husband, while seeing the wife in a subordinate role. And this relationship is to be valid " in everything," that is, in the whole of married life.

The new element here is the religious point of view. Both partners are told to live according to the order of things just laid down, by reason of their faith. The husband, following the example of Christ, is to understand his leading part as leadership on the way of salvation, the wife is to exercise her obedience as a submissive service performed towards Christ himself.

We may read here the valid and permanent religious truth that the common life of marriage is understood, religiously, as the effect of faith and of the life of grace. The image, however, which Paul has of the relationship of the sexes and the marriage partners with one another, must be taken as a mere reflection of the age he lived in. It corresponds in general to the inferior position of the woman which was maintained by the ancient world, and it reflects especially the education of Paul among the Jewish rabbis. A higher estimation of the woman, one which placed her fundamentally on the same level as the man, was just beginning to make its way in the time of Paul. The matter is perfectly clear as far as we can see, in the mind of Jesus himself. For him, from the first moment of their creation, man and woman are fully equal in the sight of God, in nature and dignity. But this truth had not as yet had any effect on practical life in apostolic times. The next verses will show that Paul himself is coming to realize the principle.

## HUSBANDS, LOVE YOUR WIVES (5:25-32)

*[25]Husbands, love your wives, as Christ also loved the Church and delivered himself up for it, [26]to sanctify it by washing it clean with water in the word, [27]so that he might himself present it glorious to himself, without stain or wrinkle or anything of the sort, that she might instead be holy and without blemish.*

Just as for wives Paul had only one thing to urge: "be subject," so the husbands, too, are provided only one fundamental precept, though it includes all others: "*love your wives!*" And once more Christ is the model: "as Christ also loved the Church and delivered himself up for it." But here, too, we are entitled to see more than a mere comparison. What Christ did for his Church should also provide the reason for the love of a husband for his wife: *because* Christ gave himself up in love for his Church, and because marriage is seen as a reflection of the relationship of Christ to the Church, *therefore* husbands should love their wives, and exercise this love in turn by a dedication ready for all sacrifices.

The end and object which Christ's sacrifice of himself upon the cross is to serve, is elsewhere mostly described as redemption from the power of darkness, as rescue from the judgment of

God's anger, or, to put it briefly, forgiveness of sins (Gal 1:4). Here, on the contrary, the positive side of this work of redemption is emphatically stressed, *sanctification,* though not so much the sanctification of the individual as the *sanctification of the Church* as a whole. This takes place through baptism, as it is applied continually to each new member of the Church.

The expression "*washing it clean with water in the word*" may be taken as an exact rendering of what theology understands by "sacrament." The "matter" is the washing in water, to which is joined the word which gives it meaning; the "form" is the baptismal formula. The Greek text has "*in* the word," which follows the Semitic usage and is the equivalent of "along with," "accompanied by."

This sanctification is now described in a series of metaphors. Christ has given himself up on the cross for the Church," to present it glorious to himself." The word "present" may be understood as almost a technical term for the "giving away" of a bride. Paul uses it of himself also when he sees himself as the "Father of the bride," the Church of Corinth, which he "presents to Christ as a pure virgin" (2 Cor 11:2). That this presentation supposes a process of formation, molding, perfecting, and making beautiful, should be clear from the way Paul speaks of his apostolic labor in the Epistle to the Colossians. He says it is done "to present each person as perfect in Christ" (1:28). What is emphasized, however, in our present text is that *Christ himself* is his own "matchmaker," as it were, who gives the Church to himself as a glorious bride. For it is he himself who makes ready the bride and causes her to be "without stain or wrinkle or anything of the sort, that she might instead be holy and without blemish." But in what sense can the Church be said to be really so glorious, pure, and stainless, and in all the fresh bloom of youth? Does it perhaps mean the Church when it has arrived at its last end, the Church perfected for eternity, wholly purified for the marriage feast of the Lamb? No, it cannot only be this, for the Church, in so far as it is the masterpiece of its bridegroom, *is* already glorious and immaculate now. What is to be made manifest one day is this very beauty which is now its own invisibly. And there is something more. Paul is thinking of the Church as it emerges from baptism, always new and gleaming and pure. It is not the Apostle's intention to speak here of what the Church then makes of itself, because he is concerned with the *aim* of Christ's sacrificial dedication and love.

*²⁸So husbands, too, should love their wives like their own body. He who loves his wife, loves himself. ²⁹For no one hates his own flesh; on the contrary, he feeds and cherishes it as Christ does the Church, ³⁰for we are members of his body.*

"*So husbands, too, should love their wives like their own body.*" The thought is not really new. It only takes up again the model provided by Christ, and stresses one aspect of his action, which had already been briefly dwelt on, when Christ was spoken of as the "saviour of his body." This implies clearly enough the idea of the love of the head for his own body, an idea which must now hold good for husbands as well: "He who loves his wife, loves himself." Paul finds in this thought a strong and clear motive why the husband should love his wife. Though put very briefly, it is still a sort of invitation to think it out and apply it in detail.

"*For no one hates his own flesh; on the contrary, he feeds and cherishes it as Christ does the Church.*" We are not bound to take " hatred " in the strong sense that it has in English. Someone is said to " hate " in the Semitic languages as soon as he shows less love to one than to another. He " hates " all the more, then, if he does not love at all, if he is neglectful of someone whom he ought to love, and meets him with coldness and indifference. What we associate with the word " hate " would only come after this, as a further degree of intensity: a real dislike, which would involve wishing actual harm to the other. Really, what is necessary is that the husband should cherish his wife the way everyone is concerned for his own bodily welfare and health, anxious to avoid all pain, careful to heal all wounds, and indeed, bent on evading all discomfort.

Once more, Christ is the model in this matter of caring and providing for his body (which is the Church). For the third time, we hear once more the insistent " *as Christ, too*," and the reason behind it, " *because Christ, too*," which gives ground for all that is demanded. We can glean from 4:16 what Paul understood by this nourishing and cherishing: " From him, the whole body is held together . . ." As love performs its service of unifying and reinforcing, *he* is really at work, intent in all upon one thing only, that this body may grow, and ripen in love towards its full maturity.

Since " feeding " is also mentioned here, we cannot be too far from the notion that Christ nourishes his body with his own very self, with his eucharistic flesh and blood, which is the visible, holds sway in us all: " for we are members of his body."

[31]" *Therefore, a man shall leave father and mother, and be joined to his wife, and the two shall become one flesh.*" [32]*This mystery is great. But I interpret it of Christ and the Church.*

³³*But in any case, each of you must love his life like himself; while the woman should fear her husband.*

Without any of the introductory formulas which Paul ordinarily uses when he appeals to a text of sacred Scripture, the passage from Genesis comes in unannounced: " Therefore, a man shall leave father and mother . . ." (Gen 2:24). This is understood as a rule primarily of marriage in the natural order. Not so by Paul. He sees here the expression of a deep mystery (" this mystery is great "), and adds the reason why he finds it a great mystery: " But I say [that it is great] in view of Christ and the Church." This seems to mean: but *I* understand it of Christ and the Church. It refers directly, of course, to the first pair of human beings. But Adam is for Paul the prefiguration (the type) of Christ, who is the Second Adam. What is said of the first must be verified more fully, and finally achieved, in the second. Thus, according to Paul, the text of Genesis really means *Christ and his marriage with the Church,* and hence it truly indicates a " great mystery."

But it is equally certain that the text also speaks of human marriage. Marriage, however, is seen as intrinsically dependent upon the all-important marriage of Christ with his Church, to which it is essentially related, since it is its reënactment. But if it is to be really a reënactment or re-accomplishment, human marriage is more than a copy or resemblance. In marriage between members of Christ, something of Christ's life-giving union with his Church must be embodied and realized. Thus marriage enters not merely as an image, but as part of the process, into what Paul calls the basic mystery: Christ the bridegroom, forming one body with his bride, the Church. This is what allows us now to regard marriage as part of the mystery, as a means of grace, and therefore as a sacrament. That it has this character precisely as an image of the union of *the* great bridegroom with his bride, the Church, makes this sacrament different from the others, and gives it its own independent character.

After this deep insight into the mystery of *Christian marriage* —for in the end, this is all that comes into his horizon—Paul returns in conclusion to the basic admonition which he gave to married people at the start. We should expect, after all that has gone before, that the final exhortation would begin with the word " therefore " or the like, and so be recognizable as the result or consequence of the preceding. The Apostle, however, rather surprisingly introduces the final sentence with the word " but." The conjunction expresses, no doubt, one of the aims of the preceding passage. It is as though Paul wished to say: whether you have followed this argument or not, the important thing is that you *do* the right thing: " But in any case, each of you must love his wife like himself; while the woman should fear her husband," that is, be full of respect for her husband in all their encounters.

## Children and Parents (6:1-4)

### CHILDREN, OBEY YOUR PARENTS (6:1-3)

¹*Children, obey your parents, in the Lord, for that is right. " Honor your father and your mother "—this is a first commandment, with a promise—*³*so that it may be well with you and that you may live long upon earth.*

The addition of "in the Lord" is textually uncertain. No doubt, it springs naturally to the mind of Paul, but it seems astonishing in an address to children. In the parallel text of the Epistle to the Colossians the reason for obedience is given in a way that is perhaps better adapted to the mind of children: "for that is well pleasing in the Lord" (Col 3:20), which could almost be rendered as: "for if you do that you will give the Lord joy." The text in Ephesians thinks more in legal terms: "for that is the right [and just] thing to do." "*Honor your father and your mother.*" The fourth commandment, however, is not to be simply repeated in its well-known form, and registered likewise only mechanically. Paul interrupts himself. He inserts the words: "that is a first commandment, with a promise." This is hardly to be understood as "the first commandment in the Decalogue, to which a promise is attached." Taken this way, it would rather be the only one of its kind in the Ten Commandments. Nor can "the first commandment" be understood as the first on the so-called Second Table. It is "a first commandment," much more probably, in the sense of its rank. The rabbis, too, held that the fourth commandment was one of the "heavy," that is, important ones. Indeed, it was looked upon as "the heaviest of the heavy." As "a first commandment," the fourth is characterized by the added promise. In a legal text above all, in an enumeration of commandments, one cannot but feel what it means when the lawgiver steps out of his role, so to speak, to add in a promise, as here: "that it may be well with you, and that you may live long upon earth." Paul is less interested in the promise as a motive than in emphasizing how God himself has thus laid a singular stress on the fourth commandment. Hence there is no point in asking how Paul understood the promise of earthly happiness and long life, which is so authentic a part of the Old Testament. He himself, in any case, was full of quite a different hope, which he brings out more strongly in the Epistle to the Ephesians than practically anywhere else (see 1:12. 18).

## Fathers, be Christian educators of your children (6:4)

... *⁴And you who are fathers, do not provoke your children to anger. Bring them up rather in discipline and instruction of the Lord.*

We have a complete parallel in the Epistle to the Colossians: " You fathers, do not irritate your children, for fear they will be disheartened " (3:21). One has only to read the rules for education given in the book of Jesus Sirach (Ecclesiasticus), which are almost terrifyingly one-sided, to measure the enormous progress which Paul's *consideration for the child* means. There education or " discipline " is almost the equivalent of corporal chastisement, and the only motive given for a good, that is, a decidedly severe upbringing, is not, as one might expect, the good of the child. It is to provide the father with an untroubled and honored old age. When one starts from there, and comes upon the Pauline admonition, " Fathers, do not provoke your children," one feels oneself in the springtime of a new age, in the sphere of education.

The child should not be the victim of his father's moodiness. What provokes to anger, exasperates and embitters, is an undisciplined, selfish nature, behind which there is only a miserable ego, but no great love. Paul supposes in the child a delicate sense of what is just, what stems from real love, even though it be severe. He therefore warns against behavior that could leave children "disgusted" with their father, that could prejudice them against him and against everything contained in the word "father." The loss has graver consequences than might appear at first sight. For "father" should not be a mere concept, but a whole world, a world of goodness, warmth, and strength, and of security in this strength. What the father has been to the child, so too will the *heavenly Father* appear, when the child is taught to pray, "Our Father . . ." Where else could he learn what "father" means, if not from his own deep experience at the time when he is most receptive? Is every Christian father aware of this responsibility?

". . . *Bring them up rather in discipline and instruction of the Lord.*" The two expressions have a predominantly severe tone in the language of sacred Scripture. They could be translated by "discipline and correction." Or they could almost suggest an education by means of chastisement and rebuke. However, there is something new, and it is decisive: the addition of "in the Lord." This means that parents are to bring up their children with the wisdom of a "Christian" educator, giving them a training in which Christ, his person, and his work are the motivation, the model to follow, and finally the goal to attain.

One could regret the fact that there is no mention of the *mother* here. Are children to be brought up without the wife having a large share in it, precisely in her role of mother? The fact is that the place of the woman, even in the mind of Paul, with his Jewish background, was not that which it has become in the course of many centuries of Christian culture. In almost losing sight of the woman, a phenomenon which occurs elsewhere as well in Paul, he is undoubtedly a child of his times.

On the other hand, there is still this to be said about our text:

the mother is not totally absent. She appears at the beginning on the same footing, as it were, as the man, under the common designation of " parents "—" Children, obey your parents!" And if Paul only speaks subsequently of the " fathers," who are not to exasperate their children, that may be because such an admonition appeared less urgent with regard to the mothers. And if, finally, these fathers are recommended to adopt a Christian way of education, it is undoubtedly because the father's seriousness, and a certain strictness on his part, are in fact the backbone, more or less, of the bringing up of children. The wife, however, who is one with her husband through her assent to his decisions, will not fail to do her part by her motherly tenderness, a gift which she alone possesses. And further: how much is gained, even for the children, by that silent, self-sacrificing, self-forgetful service of the mother! This is the way in which the mother guarantees peace in the family, and provides a home for the children in the real sense of the word.

*Slaves and Masters (6:5–9)*

### Slaves, obey in your masters Christ (6:5-8)

*⁵You who are slaves, obey your earthly masters in fear and trembling, in the simplicity of your hearts as though Christ, ⁶not just in what comes under the eye, as though you wished to please men, but as slaves of Christ, who do the will of God from the heart, ⁷serving cheerfully as though it were for the Lord and not [just] men, ⁸knowing well that each one, if he does something good, will be rewarded for it by the Lord, whether he be a slave or free.*

There is still a word to be directed to slaves and masters, to complete the "list of household duties," namely, the instruction of the "family," in the ancient sense of the word. From slaves, then, Paul demands a concept of their "calling" which is very high indeed. Only the founders of religious orders in later times have dared to demand such a profound obedience, but then it was from subjects who submitted themselves freely to superiors set over them by God. One must have attempted it oneself, in this very different situation, in order properly to admire the spirit of faith which Paul seems to take for granted in the simplest and often totally uneducated Christians. Just as the woman is to see Christ in her husband and so submit to him, so too the slave is to obey Christ in his master, not only when things go well, but also when the master is vexatious (see I Pet 2:18). Paul calls for "*holy awe*": that is what is meant by the biblical expression "in fear and trembling," and by the addition "in simplicity of heart."

This *simplicity* is to be understood in the most original sense of the word. It is the condition of the inward man which knows only one *goal*, a goal he serves without other ends in view, concentrating on it all his strength and all his devotion. So the slave is to see in his master Christ alone, to whom he lovingly dedicates all his energies. They are to recognize themselves as slaves of Christ, and do the will of their masters "from the heart," which is precisely the type of service which only can be done for God, since it comes from the depths of the soul. The opposite would be just a sort of "lip service," meaning here, an effort to please men, a service that goes only as far as the watchful eye of the master can see. Such would be the "two-track minds" (in contrast to the "simple hearts," which could be called, in a good sense, "one-track minds"), divided between their forced labor and the wish of their own hearts. The " slave of Christ " must not be one of these.

Paul repeats his main thought, thereby acknowledging that what he demands is not at all easy. They are to serve "*cheerfully*," because they serve the Lord, and not simply men. And here the thought of the reward occurs once more. In the last resort, they are really working for their own benefit as well, no matter how much they seem to be the mere instruments of someone else's will. It is as true of them as of anybody else: " Whatever good one does, one will receive back from the Lord . . ."

## Masters, think of the one true Lord (6:9)

*⁹And you who are masters, behave towards them in the same way. Give up threatening, since you know that their and your Lord is in heaven, and that the rank of the person has no value in his eyes.*

". . . *behave towards them in the same way.*" The seeming looseness of expression is significant here. Slaves are to give their masters service and obedience. Are the masters to do something of the same kind for their slaves? No, Paul is not thinking of the different conduct of slaves and masters; he is totally preoccupied by the thought of what is really common to both: that absolutely everything they do should be for the Lord and not for men. How completely Paul is dominated by this thought may be seen from the fact that he automatically demands of both of them that they should " do the same thing." If so, the masters will not scold, threaten, or shout, because they know that in reality there is only one who is *the* Lord, to whom slaves and masters alike belong; and that the only thing that counts before his judgment seat is the " good done " by each, or the evil, " whether he be slave or free."

Paul has addressed himself to wives and husbands, children and parents, slaves and masters. The *sequence* here is remarkable, because even as a mere matter of language and usage we find it hard to speak of " wife and husband " instead of " husband and wife." The same is true of the two other pairs. The sequence is obviously not determined by dignity and rank, but by the greater necessity in each case, of the exhortation, " be subject "! Paul felt that it should be the guiding principle of an exemplary family life. Of the three pairs, it is always the *subordinate member* which Paul addresses in the first place. This may be connected with his proclamation of a new freedom, of the abolition of all differences in Christ, where there is no longer " circumcised or uncircumcised, barbarian, Scythian, slave, or free, but only Christ who is all in all " (Col 3:11). Or, as in the Epistle to the Galatians, in a passage which corresponds even better to our present text: " It means nothing any longer to be Jew or Greek, slave or free, male or female, for you are all one person in Christ Jesus " (Gal 3:28).

## Put on the Armor of God (6:10-22)

### *God's Armor Is Necessary (6:10-13)*

[10]*For the rest, finally, grow strong in the Lord, and in the force of his might.* [11]*Put on the armor of God, that you may be able to stand firm against the stratagems of the devil;* [12]*for our fight*

*is not against flesh and blood, but against the authorities and powers, against the world rulers of this darkness, against the spirits of wickedness in the heavens.* ¹³*Therefore, take up the armor of God, that you may be able to resist on the evil day, and when you have accomplished everything, stand firm [as victors].*

Paul begins this section with a formula (" for the rest, finally "), which writers liked to use to pass on to the conclusion. His language now takes wings. He has to make his farewells, who knows for how long. " So grow strong, then, in the Lord, and in the force of his might." The Apostle would like to have his faithful equipped with all the power of God. What is in front of them is not tranquility and security, but a *fight,* and for that they have to be armed. But these arms must come from God, if everything is to turn out well. If it were a struggle between human beings, then human forces could be relied upon for help. But now a completely different set of enemies have taken the field.

Once more we come forward upon the " powers," " forces," and " authorities " who were spoken of at the very beginning of the epistle, when Paul was acclaiming the exhaltation of Christ, the risen Lord, high above all angelic powers (1:21). There the question of the nature of these powers was left undecided. Now they are presented openly as the powers hostile to God, who are in the service of Satan, and hence are expressly called " spirits of wickedness." They hurl themselves against the followers of him who has conquered them radically on the cross. And their despairing rage is all the wilder, the shorter the time they know they have, and the more futile their effort: whenever they clash with him who has mastered them—which is really all they ever do. For it is Christ who is ultimately " the armor of God," no matter what its component parts may be called: breastplate, shield, helmet, or sword.

The equipment provided by God is ready, but *it has to be put on*, and it is for each one to do this. Hence Paul says once more: " So, take up the armor of God, so that on the evil day "—which is the " Time of the End," when Christians must reckon with a final revolt of the defeated enemies of God—" so that on the evil day you may be able to resist, and emerge as victors, after you have accomplished everything." The last phrase can mean: after you have overcome all enemies. But it can also mean: after you have performed everything that lies in your power. The victory is God's, but the truth is that he wishes to gain this victory by fighting the battle through Jesus Christ and along with you.

## *What the Armor of God Consists of* (6:14–17)

<sup>14</sup>*Therefore stand firm, your loins girded with [the] truth, equipped with the breastplate of justice* <sup>15</sup>*and your feet shod with readiness for the Gospel of peace.* <sup>16</sup>*In all things, take up the shield of faith, with which you will be able to quench all the fiery darts of the wicked one.* <sup>17</sup>*And take the helmet of salvation and the sword of the Spirit, which is the word of God, . . .*

For the third time, Paul starts off with the same appeal. One can almost feel how impressed he is by the greatness of the danger, and how much he fears that it may be underestimated. For invisible powers are engaged; there are " stratagems " (" methods " is the Greek word) of the devil, which have to be parried. *Deviousness and craftiness* are characteristic of his tactics. These spiritual powers are world rulers " in darkness," in the region of the invisible and impalpable, and they like nothing better than to be unrecognized, to wear a thousand masks and remain disguised.

It would not be right to ask in each of the following instances, why precisely truth appears linked with the belt, justice with the coat-of-mail, peace with the shoes, faith with the shield, salvation with the helmet, and the word of God with the sword. Paul is only interested in the general picture of the armament provided by God. He must, therefore, be thinking of gifts of God in the strictest sense, when he speaks here of truth, justice, peace, and faith as part of this military equipment.

" *Girded with [the] truth,"* therefore, means the truth of which it was said in 1:13: "In him you have heard the word of truth, the good tidings of your salvation." It is the truth which it is the Christian's duty to live out in love (4:15).

" . . . *equipped with the breastplate of justice."* The same image of justice as a breastplate is found also in the Old Testament, but there it is God himself who equips himself for war with his justice. So the biblical echo is audible in our text, but the *justice* spoken of is quite different. Here it is the justice which God confers upon a Christian, and the only justice which has value in his eyes. It is the justice which stands in opposition to one's own justice, gained by fidelity to the Law. Paul makes this distinction, for instance, in the Epistle to the Philippians, when he writes: "I strive hard to be in Christ, not in virtue of *my own* justice, which stems from the Law, but with the justice which stems from faith in Jesus Christ, with the justice which comes from God, by reason of faith " (3:9). When, on the other hand, in the First Epistle to the Thessalonians, it is not justice which appears as breastplate, but faith and love (5:8), this only shows how freely Paul makes use of his imagery, and therefore that they are not to be pressed.

"... *shod with readiness for the Gospel of peace.*" Paul obviously has in mind the text of Isaiah: " How welcome on the mountains are the feet of the herald of joy, who proclaims peace and brings good tidings and whose message is salvation " (52:7). This unmistakeable allusion to the text of the prophet suggests that we are not to understand by the words " *readiness of the Gospel* " a readiness such as the Gospel confers. It must rather be readiness to proclaim the Gospel of peace—which is done by preaching Christ who " is our peace," because he united the hostile brothers in himself as a new man, reconciling them with the Father (2:14-17). The allusion to this basic peacemaking is all the clearer since Paul's account of Christ's work of peace (ch. 2) ends with the words of Isaiah: " And he has proclaimed peace to those who are far off, and peace to those who are near " (Is 57:19).

This readiness to proclaim the Gospel is the only item in the whole military equipment which manifests an urge to take the offensive and make conquests: all the rest rather points to successful defense. Here it is significant that it is precisely peace which becomes the weapon against the powers of darkness. *Their* efforts are bent upon hostility and discord, and every element of peace and unity in the world of men is a defeat for them.

" *In all things, take up the shield of faith.*" The word for shield here means, in contrast to the small round buckler, the great long shield which covers the soldier completely. When Paul says " in all things," he is probably thinking of the fundamental importance of the faith, with its bearing upon all matters. We are reminded of 2:8: " By faith are you saved—through faith. And this is not from you, God's is the gift."

Here we have the only indication of *the effects of the weapons*. With the shield of faith, " you will be able to quench all the fiery darts of the evil one." One would expect the shield to " deflect " the darts. When in spite of this Paul says that it " quenches " them, it only shows what is the real danger, as he sees it. He is not interested in keeping to the metaphor, but he knows that the darts are fiery, and that fire spreads. In the next phrase, " *helmet of salvation,*" salvation means no doubt the gifts of salvation, the hope of full salvation, to which we are called. Paul lays great stress upon this in the Epistle to the Ephesians particularly. We may recall how earlier he had prayed for his friends that they might have " the eyes of the heart illumined," that they might be fully aware of how great is the hope to which God called them (1:18). And when later the whole moral exhortation to Christian living is placed under the heading, " walk worthy of the call which you have received " (4:1), that means for Paul behaving like men from whose whole life it is manifest that they are travelling towards an overwhelming glory. Thus hope, and the thankful joy of the heart which goes with it, is really a protection against temptation and assault, and can well be compared to a helmet that resists all blows. The sword is *"the word of God,"* and it is the Spirit that makes of it an effective weapon. The Spirit has given us the word of God, and he alone has the power to make it a force in our lives. The word of God is often called a sword, in the Old Testament as well as the New. John contemplates Christ in a grandiose vision with " a sword going forth from his mouth, two-edged and sharp " (Rev 1:16), and in the Epistle to the Hebrews we have the well-known text: " The word of God is full of life and force, and sharper than a two-edged sword. It pierces to the division between soul, spirit, joint, and marrow, and is judge of the deepest thoughts and stirrings of the heart " (4:12).

For us the " word of God " is above all the word of *sacred Scripture*. If it is to be a sword, it must be wielded. But this calls for perseverance and tireless practice. The word of Scripture must be at hand, first of all. That means we must know it and have made it our most intimate and vital possession. The next thing is to know all the feints of Satan, and be ready for each of them with the right counter attack. The Lord himself has shown us how it is to be done, in his passage of arms with Satan, which has been recorded in our Gospels (Mt 4:1-11).

## *Request for Unceasing Prayer (6:18–22)*

### PRAYER IS NEEDED, IN BEHALF OF ALL CHRISTIANS AND THE APOSTLE (6:18–20)

... *[18]with wholehearted prayer and entreaty. Pray on all occasions in the Spirit, and stay awake for this, with all perseverance and all manner of prayer for all the saints [19]and for me that words may be granted me, when I open my mouth, to proclaim the mystery of the Gospel with frankness, [20]for which I am an ambassador in chains, so that I may speak frankly in his service, as I ought to speak.*

In very close conjunction with the foregoing, Paul goes on to ask his faithful to help him with their prayers. This remarkably close link-up makes us suspect that for Paul prayer also plays an important part in the armament of God. On the other hand, he now drops the military metaphors, unless one still wishes to hear an echo of it in the summons to "watch." Paul is exigent. The Christian fighter must take the field as one who practices "every sort of prayer," thanksgiving, praise, and vehement intercession; as one who prays "on *all* occasions," "in *every* situation," and therefore, always; as one for whom the whole day is not enough for prayer, and who therefore stays awake at night and devotes himself to prayer "with all perseverance." What are we to understand by "*all* perseverance," "*all sorts* of persistance"? Perhaps the author himself does not know. He is simply eager to say "all" and "every" three times over, in order to grip his Christian reader, wholly and entirely, all his time, all his strength, all his efforts down to the last.

Paul often comes to speak of this *unceasing prayer* in his epistles. He practices it himself: ". . . and so we pray earnestly day and night " (1 Thes 3:10). He mentions his night vigils along with his labors and his fasts (2 Cor 6:5). He remembers Timothy constantly "day and night in his prayers" (2 Tim 1:3). And it is certainly no empty formula when he so often begins his letters with the assurance: "I never cease to pray for you" (1:16). He desires, therefore, a like return from his Christian friends: "Be joyful always, pray without interruption, give thanks in every situation, for that is what God wants from you in Jesus Christ " (1 Thes 5:16-18). It is the same in our present text.

*How are they to pray?* Paul says: "in the Spirit." What he means by that, we can see from the Epistle to the Romans: "The Spirit aids our weakness. For we do not know what we should ask for, to do it well. But he, the Spirit, intercedes for us with wordless sighs. He who searches the heart knows what is the desire of our spirit, since he pleads for the saints according to the mind of God" (Rom 8:26f.). Paul therefore means prayer which is void of all self-will and which fits in with the intentions of God himself. It listens intently to the inner voice, it obeys every inspiration of the Spirit, and at the same time puts its whole confidence in this divine prayer within us—which will not, however, deprive itself of our prayer.

The object of this prayer is to be "all the saints" and the Apostle himself. *"For all the saints"* means in behalf of the people of God, for the Church, the body of Christ, asking that it may grow outwardly and inwardly, and ripen towards its maturity. This growth, as we have seen (4:16), derives from the head, from Christ. But Christ builds up his body through the "achievements" of each member for each other and for the whole. Paul is convinced that this "achievement" is accomplished to a great extent in the form of prayer of intercession.

He knows that he himself is dependent upon it. This may appear surprising, in view of all the "grace of state" which was bestowed upon him for his apostolic office. It is nonetheless true. Here as elsewhere, he turns to the faithful, as though he were helpless without their prayers, as though it depended upon their prayers that the right words might be given him at the proclamation of the Gospel, and—something rare—that he might find the courage (!) to speak as boldly as God and his calling demand of him (Col 4:2-4). Does this tinge of anxiety about a possible lack of outspokenness arise from his situation as a prisoner? That we do not know. But in any case, he reminds his readers of his present situation. He does so, however, rather proudly, with the reminder that "I am an ambassador in chains," for the mystery which after all is Christ himself.

But this section shows us, above all things else, what *life in and with the Church means* in practice for Paul. We see how he pictures his Christians. He sees them in perpetual conversation with God in prayer. One would think that they are preoccupied in their thoughts, desires, and cares, only with the weal and woe of the Church, whose members they know they are. Paul here presupposes in each individual a profound sense of belonging to the community, a really lively sense of sharing in everything that goes on in the whole, a way of thinking in terms of the community which must put us present-day members of the great Church to shame. At that time it was still true: each for all and all for each, with no one thinking only in his own trifling, personal interests. What challenges the Christian is too great. How should it not then claim the whole of him? For it makes this little life of the individual great and important, important for time and for the eternity to come, important for us and for the others who are our brothers, important—and this is supreme —for him to whom we owe all, and to whom, therefore, all our love is due.

## Hence Tychicus is to bring news of him (6:21–22)

*²¹But in order that you, too, may know about my situation, how things are with me, Tychicus, the beloved brother and loyal helper in the Lord, will give you all the news. ²²I am sending him to you for this very reason, that you may learn all about us, and that he may comfort your hearts.*

Paul introduces Tychicus not as "*my* beloved brother," but as "*the beloved brother*." He is to be the beloved brother for the receivers of the epistle also. It is no less of a recommendation that he is a "loyal helper in the Lord," one of those upon whom Paul can rely to take up any burden for the sake of the Gospel. He will bring news of the Apostle, and in addition, " comfort " for their hearts, which is the encouragement that the Christian heart always needs again and again: someone who will console and exhort, spur it on and give it courage. The Apostle has done the best he can in this line in the epistle, which is now at an end. He cannot himself come, but he sends someone from his closest circle of friends. Tychicus was there while Paul was thinking out this letter, and it is even possible that he actually wrote it down as the master dictated it, as Tertius did the Epistle to the Romans. He is now to give the written word something of the living voice, into which the heart-beat of the Apostle has entered.

# THE ENDING OF THE LETTER

# THE BLESSING (6:23-24)

²²*Peace to the brothers and love with faith from God the Father and the Lord Jesus Christ.* ²³*[May] grace [be] with all who love our Lord Jesus Christ in immortality.*

The epistle ends, like all the other epistles by *wishing a blessing*. And yet it is somewhat different. Elsewhere we mostly find personal greetings, like old friends waving to each other when they part. There is no such personal acquaintanceship here, and the prayer for a blessing has a solemnity that makes it rather reserved. But it remains essentially what it is, and it goes deep.

Paul wishes the community *peace*. We have already noted that this was the formula of greeting used in the East. It is a general wish for all that we should call "welfare." This concept of welfare or salvation had been enriched in Judaism by the hope of the times of the Messiah, and this peace of Christ became part of the vocabulary of the early Church, in the sense of "salvation achieved." The epistle has spoken expressly and forcibly of this peace of Christ, indeed of Christ who "is our peace" (2:14). Now this peace should make its full effect felt upon the brothers, with all the blessings it brings.

In addition, the Apostle wishes them *"love with faith."* It is love that should "preserve the unity of the Spirit in the bond of peace" (4:3); love that should lend them the strength to be patient and forgiving (4:2); love that is so truly the creative force in the construction and the expansion of the body of Christ

(4:16). But that is only possible to a love which grows from faith and finds ever new support in faith, which is indeed at root nothing else than faith translated into life (4:15). This faith is the gift of God (2:8), and love is no less a gift, for in this love there is, after all, nothing but the love of Christ as it goes into action (4:16). Hence it can be truly said: "love with faith from God the Father and the Lord Jesus Christ."

Finally, Paul sums up everything that he can wish them as the *grace* in which we are saved (2:8), which leads us in the Holy Spirit towards the definitive redemption (1:14), in which it will then be revealed as splendor, for the glory of God (2:7).

The Apostle wishes this to those "*who love our Lord Jesus Christ.*" This sounds like a sort of transcription for the word "Christians." But this final recall of the love of the faithful for Christ is very precious, because it is remarkably rare in Paul. His epistles are full of the love of Christ for us. Numerous texts bear eloquent testimony to the Apostle's own love for Christ, but without referring the verb "love" expressly to Christ as the object of love (see Phil 1:23). Apart from the present text, the only place in which Paul speaks expressly of the love of the faithful for Christ is at the end of the First Epistle to the Corinthians: "If anyone does not love the Lord, let him be under a ban" (16:22). In all the rest of the New Testament epistles, the only other text to be mentioned would be the First Epistle of Peter. It is the text which comes closest to that of the Ephesians: "You love him indeed, though you have not seen him" (1:8).

But there is still one last word in the epistle. It is a pity that it remains obscure for us: "*in immortality,*" literally, "in imperishability." The word is the equivalent of "eternal life." The expression "in eternal life" should, no doubt, be referred to those who love Christ, who according to this very epistle already have a share in eternal life, and are already " enthroned in the heavens in Christ Jesus," as Paul so boldly put it (2:6). Or we can refer the expression to Christ, whom the faithful love " in his majesty." In either case, we should have something which is very fitting for the conclusion of this epistle: a resumption of its beginning, which praised God for all the blessings with which he has blessed us " *in heaven* in Christ " (1:3). He has blessed us, indeed, but—let us not forget—for the praise of the glory of his grace, with which he has favored us in his Beloved (1:6).